Individual Studies
for Grade 2

*A Year of Lesson Plans
for Language Arts, Math, and Science*

by
Sonya Shafer

Individual Studies for Grade 2: A Year of Lesson Plans for Language Arts, Math, and Science
© 2015, Sonya Shafer

Cover Design: John Shafer and Sarah Shafer

ISBN 978-1-61634-308-8 printed
ISBN 978-1-61634-309-5 electronic download

Published by
Simply Charlotte Mason, LLC
930 New Hope Road #11-892
Lawrenceville, Georgia 30045
simplycharlottemason.com

Printed by PrintLogic, Inc.
Monroe, Georgia, USA

Contents

How to Use

Most school subjects can be taught to your whole family together, but some subjects are best taught individually so you can progress at the student's pace. This book of lesson plans contains suggestions and assignments for individual work for students in grade 2. Complete one lesson plan per day to finish these studies in a school year.

The lesson plans in this book cover reading and writing, science, and math.

Reading & Writing

Since students at this young age vary greatly in readiness for reading and writing, we offer two tracks of plans: A and B. Select the track that best fits your student and follow that track's plans throughout the year.

Track A—For students who can already read many words and short sentences and can print letters but need more practice reading and writing to gain fluency.

Track B—For students who would benefit from more reading practice and who are ready to learn cursive.

Science

Science can be done individually, or if you have more than one student in grades 1–6, they may all do one science course together. Simply Charlotte Mason has several to choose from.

Nature Study is an important part of science studies; be sure to include it. Follow the Nature Study suggestions in your selected science course or use the nature notebook, *Journaling a Year in Nature*, to guide your weekly study. Nature Study can be done all together as a family, but we have included reminders in these individual plans too.

Math

Use the math curriculum of your choice. These lesson plans will include reminders to work on it. As with other individual work, be sure to go at your student's pace.

Complete Year's Resources List

- Math course of choice
- Simply Charlotte Mason science course of choice
- *Journaling a Year in Nature* notebooks, one per person (optional)

Select Track A *or Track B*

Track A
- *Busy Times*
- *More Busy Times*
- *A Child's Copybook Reader,* Volumes 1–3
    The copybook readers are available in two handwriting styles: the traditional print-straight-up-and-down Zaner Bloser and the print-on-a-slant D'Nealian. Select whichever style you prefer.

Track B
- *New Friends*
- *More New Friends*
- *Print to Cursive Proverbs*
    Print to Cursive Proverbs is available in two handwriting styles: the traditional print-straight-up-and-down Zaner Bloser and the print-on-a-slant D'Nealian. Select whichever style your student has learned to print in.

Note: All resources except math are available from Simply Charlotte Mason.

Term 1
(12 weeks; 5 lessons/week)

Term 1 Resources List
- Math course of choice
- Simply Charlotte Mason (SCM) science course of choice
- *Journaling a Year in Nature* notebooks (optional)

Track A
- *A Child's Copybook Reader, Volume 1*
- *Busy Times*

Track B
- *Print to Cursive Proverbs*
- *New Friends*

Weekly Schedule

	Day One	Day Two	Day Three	Day Four	Day Five
	Math (15–20 min.)	Math (15–20 min.)	Math (15–20 min.)	Math (15–20 min.)	Math (15–20 min.)
		Science (15–20 min.)		Science (15–20 min.)	(Nature Study)
Track A	Copybook Reader (5 min.)	Copybook Reader (5 min.)	Copybook Reader (5 min.)	Copybook Reader (5 min.)	Busy Times (10–15 min.)
Track B	New Friends (10–15 min.)	Print to Cursive Proverbs (5–10 min.)	New Friends (10–15 min.)	Print to Cursive Proverbs (5–10 min.)	Print to Cursive Proverbs (5–10 min.)

me as 3rd grade Track A

Lesson 1

Materials Needed
- *A Child's Copybook Reader, Volume 1* (Track A)
- *New Friends* (Track B)
- Math course of choice

Track A: Help your student read aloud *A Child's Copybook Reader, Volume 1*, page 4.

Track B: Have your student read aloud *New Friends*, pages 6–14, "Something Special."

Math: Work on your selected math curriculum for 15–20 minutes.

Tip: Select either Track A or Track B to complete with your student. You need do only one. See page 7 for detailed descriptions.

Lesson 2

Materials Needed
- *A Child's Copybook Reader, Volume 1* (Track A)
- *Print to Cursive Proverbs* (Track B)
- Math course of choice
- SCM science course of choice

Track A: Have your student carefully copy *A Child's Copybook Reader, Volume 1*, page 5. Encourage him to pay close attention as he copies, for when he is done you will ask him how to spell one of the words. When he has finished the copywork, invite him first to spell any word he remembers from the passage. Ask him to spell *and*; if he is unsure, allow him to look at the word.

Track B: Have your student read aloud the proverb in *Print to Cursive Proverbs*, pages 5 and 6, then carefully copy it. Encourage him to pay close attention as he copies, for when he is done you will ask him how to spell one of the words. When he has finished the copywork, invite him first to spell any word he remembers from the passage. Ask him to spell *work*; if he is unsure, allow him to look at the word.

Tip: Feel free to jot down his selected words over in the Notes column so you can easily refer to them for periodic reviews.

Math: Work on your selected math curriculum for 15–20 minutes.

Science: In your SCM science course, complete the first assignment for Week 1. Check the suggested schedule in the course book.

Lesson 3

Materials Needed
- *A Child's Copybook Reader, Volume 1* (Track A)
- *New Friends* (Track B)
- Math course of choice

Track A: Have your student carefully copy *A Child's Copybook Reader, Volume 1*, page 6. Remind him to pay close attention as he copies, for when he is done you will ask him how to spell one of the words. When he has finished the copywork, invite him first to spell any word he remembers. Ask him to spell *all*; if he is unsure, allow him to look at the word.

Track B: Have your student read aloud *New Friends*, pages 15–21, "Something Special (Part 2)."

Math: Work on your selected math curriculum for 15–20 minutes.

Tip: You may complete school assignments in any order that works best for your family's schedule. Try to sequence lessons throughout the day to use different parts of the student's brain and body as you go along. In other words, don't schedule two "book-heavy" assignments back to back. Put the math assignment in between or do some Family work—such as Picture Study or Music Study—in between to break up the readings. Each lesson plan in this book is sequenced to help you with that important principle.

Lesson 4

Materials Needed
- *A Child's Copybook Reader, Volume 1* (Track A)
- *Print to Cursive Proverbs* (Track B)
- SCM science course of choice
- Math course of choice

Track A: Have your student carefully copy *A Child's Copybook Reader, Volume 1*, page 7. When he has finished the copywork, invite him to spell any word he remembers. Ask him to spell *things*; if he is unsure, allow him to look at the word.

Track B: Have your student read aloud the proverb at the top of *Print to Cursive Proverbs*, page 7, then complete the page.

Science: In your SCM science course, complete the second assignment for Week 1.

Math: Work on your selected math curriculum for 15–20 minutes.

Tip: If you are not able to complete the math lesson in 15–20 minutes, you can schedule another 15- or 20-minute time slot later in the day to finish (if you think it is necessary to do so).

Lesson 5

Materials Needed
- Math course of choice
- *Busy Times* (Track A)
- *Print to Cursive Proverbs* (Track B)
- *Journaling a Year in Nature* notebooks (optional)

Math: Work on your selected math curriculum for 15–20 minutes.

Track A: Help your student read aloud *Busy Times*, pages 6–16, "A Warm Day."

Tip: Don't worry if your student doesn't get through all of pages 6–16. There is a scheduled catch-up time in lesson 8.

Track B: Have your student read aloud the proverb in *Print to Cursive Proverbs*, pages 8 and 9, then carefully copy it. Remind him to pay close attention as he copies, for when he is done you will ask him how to spell one of the words. When he has finished the copywork, invite him first to spell any word he remembers. Ask him to spell *good*; if he is unsure, allow him to look at the word.

Nature Study: Take the whole family outside for nature study.

Tip: Follow the Nature Study suggestions in your SCM science course or use the nature notebooks, Journaling a Year in Nature, *to guide your weekly nature study.*

Lesson 6

Materials Needed
- *A Child's Copybook Reader, Volume 1* (Track A)
- *New Friends* (Track B)
- Math course of choice

Track A: Have your student carefully copy *A Child's Copybook Reader, Volume 1*, page 8. When he has finished the copywork, invite him to spell any word he remembers. Ask him to spell *them*; if he is unsure, allow him to look at the word.

Tip: Feel free to jot down his selected words over in the Notes column so you can easily refer to them for periodic reviews.

Track B: Have your student read aloud *New Friends*, pages 22–30, "What Is a Habit?"

Math: Work on your selected math curriculum for 15–20 minutes.

Lesson 7

Materials Needed
- *A Child's Copybook Reader, Volume 1* (Track A)
- *Print to Cursive Proverbs* (Track B)
- Math course of choice
- SCM science course of choice

Track A: Help your student read aloud *A Child's Copybook Reader, Volume 1*, page 9.

Track B: Have your student read aloud the proverb at the top of *Print to Cursive Proverbs*, page 10, then complete the page.

Math: Work on your selected math curriculum for 15–20 minutes.

Science: In your SCM science course, complete the first assignment for Week 2.

Tip: Oral narration lays the foundation for solid composition skills. Make sure your student is giving several oral narrations each week from his history, science, geography, or Bible readings. (Download the free e-book, Five Steps to Successful Narration, *at* simplycm.com/fivesteps *for helpful how-to's.)*

Lesson 8

Materials Needed
- *A Child's Copybook Reader, Volume 1* (Track A)
- *Busy Times*, if needed (Track A)
- *New Friends* (Track B)
- Math course of choice

Track A: Have your student carefully copy *A Child's Copybook Reader, Volume 1*, page 10. When he has finished the copywork, invite him to spell any word he remembers. Ask him to spell *each*; if he is unsure, allow him to look at the word.

Help your student finish reading aloud *Busy Times*, pages 6–16, "A Warm Day," if needed.

Track B: Have your student read aloud *New Friends*, pages 30–40, "Dad Keeps His Promise."

Math: Work on your selected math curriculum for 15–20 minutes.

Lesson 9

Materials Needed
- *A Child's Copybook Reader, Volume 1* (Track A)
- *Print to Cursive Proverbs* (Track B)
- SCM science course of choice
- Math course of choice

Track A: Have your student carefully copy *A Child's Copybook Reader, Volume 1*, page 11. When he has finished the copywork, invite him to spell any word he remembers. Ask him to spell *that*; if he is unsure, allow him to look at the word.

Tip: Encourage the habits of attention and best effort in copywork lessons by expecting it to be done right the first time. Mistakes or sloppy work requires the student to recopy the entire passage until it is done well.

Track B: Have your student read aloud the proverb in *Print to Cursive Proverbs*, pages 11 and 12, then carefully copy it. When he has finished the copywork, invite him to spell any word he remembers. Ask him to spell *come*; if he is unsure, allow him to look at the word.

Science: In your SCM science course, complete the second assignment for Week 2.

Math: Work on your selected math curriculum for 15–20 minutes.

Lesson 10

Materials Needed
- Math course of choice
- *Busy Times* (Track A)
- *Print to Cursive Proverbs* (Track B)
- *Journaling a Year in Nature* notebooks (optional)

Math: Work on your selected math curriculum for 15–20 minutes.

Track A: Help your student read aloud *Busy Times*, pages 17–24, "A Good Dog."

Tip: Don't worry if your student doesn't get through all of pages 17–24. There is a scheduled catch-up time in lesson 12.

Track B: Have your student read aloud the proverb at the top of *Print to Cursive Proverbs*, page 13, then complete the page.

Nature Study: Take the whole family outside for nature study.

Tip: Follow the Nature Study suggestions in your SCM science course or use the nature notebooks, Journaling a Year in Nature, *to guide your weekly nature study.*

Lesson 11

Materials Needed
- *A Child's Copybook Reader, Volume 1* (Track A)
- *New Friends* (Track B)
- Math course of choice

Track A: Have your student carefully copy *A Child's Copybook Reader, Volume 1*, page 12. When he has finished the copywork, invite him to spell any word he remembers. Ask him to spell *made*; if he is unsure, allow him to look at the word.

Track B: Have your student read aloud *New Friends*, pages 41–52, "Help for Rachel's Habit."

Tip: The poems sprinkled throughout New Friends *are optional. You may have your student read them or skip them. They will not be scheduled into these plans. (We recommend you focus on one master poet for the entire year, reading aloud one of his poems each week for the whole family. Details are given in SCM's Enrichment lesson plan books and* Enjoy the Poems *series.)*

Math: Work on your selected math curriculum for 15–20 minutes.

Lesson 12

Materials Needed
- *A Child's Copybook Reader, Volume 1* (Track A)
- *Busy Times*, if needed (Track A)
- *Print to Cursive Proverbs* (Track B)
- Math course of choice
- SCM science course of choice

Track A: Help your student finish reading aloud *Busy Times*, pages 17–24, "A Good Dog," if needed.
Have your student carefully copy *A Child's Copybook Reader, Volume 1,*

page 13. When he has finished the copywork, invite him to spell any word he remembers. Ask him to spell *their*; if he is unsure, allow him to look at the word.

Tip: Many of the words that you are asking for in these gentle spelling exercises are from the 100 Most Commonly Used words your student learned in Delightful Reading.

Track B: Have your student read aloud the proverb in *Print to Cursive Proverbs*, pages 14 and 15, then carefully copy it. When he has finished the copywork, invite him to spell any word he remembers. Ask him to spell *fear*; if he is unsure, allow him to look at the word.

Math: Work on your selected math curriculum for 15–20 minutes.

Science: In your SCM science course, complete the first assignment for Week 3.

Lesson 13

Materials Needed
- *A Child's Copybook Reader, Volume 1* (Track A)
- *New Friends,* if needed (Track B)
- Math course of choice

Track A: Help your student read aloud *A Child's Copybook Reader, Volume 1*, page 14.

Track B: Use today to catch up on any assigned reading in *New Friends*, as needed.

Math: Work on your selected math curriculum for 15–20 minutes.

Lesson 14

Materials Needed
- *A Child's Copybook Reader, Volume 1* (Track A)
- *Print to Cursive Proverbs* (Track B)
- SCM science course of choice
- Math course of choice

Track A: Have your student carefully copy *A Child's Copybook Reader, Volume 1*, page 15. When he has finished the copywork, invite him to spell any word he remembers. Ask him to spell *in*; if he is unsure, allow him to look at the word.

Track B: Have your student read aloud the proverb at the top of *Print to Cursive Proverbs*, page 16, then complete the page.

Science: In your SCM science course, complete the second assignment for Week 3.

Math: Work on your selected math curriculum for 15–20 minutes.

Lesson 15

Materials Needed
- Math course of choice
- *Busy Times* (Track A)
- *Print to Cursive Proverbs* (Track B)
- *Journaling a Year in Nature* notebooks (optional)

Math: Work on your selected math curriculum for 15–20 minutes.

Track A: Help your student read aloud *Busy Times*, pages 25–34, "Rover and the Wagon."

Tip: Don't worry if your student doesn't get through all of pages 25–34. There is a scheduled catch-up time in lesson 17.

Track B: Have your student read aloud the proverb in *Print to Cursive Proverbs*, page 17, then carefully copy it. When he has finished the copywork, invite him to spell any word he remembers. Ask him to spell *before*; if he is unsure, allow him to look at the word.

Nature Study: Take the whole family outside for nature study.

Tip: Follow the Nature Study suggestions in your SCM science course or use the nature notebooks, Journaling a Year in Nature, *to guide your weekly nature study.*

Lesson 16

Materials Needed
- *A Child's Copybook Reader, Volume 1* (Track A)
- *New Friends* (Track B)
- Math course of choice

Track A: Have your student carefully copy *A Child's Copybook Reader, Volume 1*, page 16. When he has finished the copywork, invite him to spell any word he remembers. Ask him to spell *at*; if he is unsure, allow him to look at the word.

Track B: Have your student read aloud *New Friends*, pages 58–66, "Tricked By a Bird."

Math: Work on your selected math curriculum for 15–20 minutes.

Lesson 17

Materials Needed
- *A Child's Copybook Reader, Volume 1* (Track A)
- *Busy Times*, if needed (Track A)
- *Print to Cursive Proverbs,* if needed (Track B)
- Math course of choice
- SCM science course of choice

Track A: Help your student finish reading aloud *Busy Times*, pages 25–34, "Rover and the Wagon," if needed.

Have your student carefully copy *A Child's Copybook Reader, Volume 1*, page 17. When he has finished the copywork, invite him to spell any word he remembers. Ask him to spell *God*; if he is unsure, allow him to look at the word.

Track B: Use today to catch up on any assigned pages in *Print to Cursive Proverbs*, as needed. If desired, review these words and your student's selected words from previous copywork lessons: *work, good, come, fear, before*. If your student is unsure about a particular word's spelling, allow him to look at the word.

Math: Work on your selected math curriculum for 15–20 minutes.

Science: In your SCM science course, complete the first assignment for Week 4.

Lesson 18

Materials Needed
- *A Child's Copybook Reader, Volume 1* (Track A)
- *New Friends* (Track B)
- Math course of choice

Track A: Have your student carefully copy *A Child's Copybook Reader, Volume 1*, page 18. When he has finished the copywork, invite him to spell any word he remembers. If desired, review 6–10 of these words and his selected words from previous copywork lessons: *and, all, things, them, each, that, made, their, in, at, God*. If your student is unsure about a particular word's spelling, allow him to look at the word.

Tip: Don't encourage guessing during these lessons; you want him to see the word spelled correctly as much as possible.

Track B: Have your student read aloud *New Friends*, pages 66–77, "Chee, the Barn Swallow."

Math: Work on your selected math curriculum for 15–20 minutes.

Lesson 19

Materials Needed
- *A Child's Copybook Reader, Volume 1* (Track A)
- *Print to Cursive Proverbs* (Track B)
- SCM science course of choice
- Math course of choice

Track A: Help your student read aloud *A Child's Copybook Reader, Volume 1*, page 19.

Track B: Have your student read aloud the proverb at the top of *Print to Cursive Proverbs*, page 18, then complete the page.

Science: In your SCM science course, complete the second assignment for Week 4.

Math: Work on your selected math curriculum for 15–20 minutes.

Lesson 20

Materials Needed
- Math course of choice
- *Busy Times* (Track A)
- *Print to Cursive Proverbs* (Track B)
- *Journaling a Year in Nature* notebooks (optional)

Math: Work on your selected math curriculum for 15–20 minutes.

Track A: Help your student read aloud *Busy Times*, pages 36–43, "A Pet Goat."

Tip: Don't worry if your student doesn't get through all of pages 36–43. There is a scheduled catch-up time in lesson 22.

Track B: Have your student complete *Print to Cursive Proverbs*, page 19.

Nature Study: Take the whole family outside for nature study.

Lesson 21

Materials Needed
- *A Child's Copybook Reader, Volume 1* (Track A)
- *New Friends* (Track B)
- Math course of choice

Track A: Have your student carefully copy *A Child's Copybook Reader, Volume 1*, page 20. When he has finished the copywork, invite him to spell any word he remembers. Ask him to spell *the*; if he is unsure, allow him to look at the word.

Track B: Have your student read aloud *New Friends*, pages 78–83, "Peggy, the Penguin."

Math: Work on your selected math curriculum for 15–20 minutes.

Lesson 22

Materials Needed
- *A Child's Copybook Reader, Volume 1* (Track A)
- *Busy Times*, if needed (Track A)
- *Print to Cursive Proverbs* (Track B)
- Math course of choice
- SCM science course of choice

Track A: Help your student finish reading aloud *Busy Times*, pages 36–43, "A Pet Goat," if needed.

Have your student carefully copy *A Child's Copybook Reader, Volume 1*, page 21. When he has finished the copywork, invite him to spell any word he remembers. Ask him to spell *run* and to look closely and tell how the word changes when *ing* is added to the end. Ask him to spell *running*; if he is unsure, allow him to look at the word.

Track B: Have your student read aloud the proverb in *Print to Cursive Proverbs*, page 20, then carefully copy it. When he has finished the copywork, invite him to spell any word he remembers. Ask him to spell *turns*; if he is unsure, allow him to look at the word.

Math: Work on your selected math curriculum for 15–20 minutes.

Science: In your SCM science course, complete the first assignment for Week 5.

Lesson 23

Materials Needed
- *A Child's Copybook Reader, Volume 1* (Track A)
- *New Friends* (Track B)
- Math course of choice

Track A: Have your student carefully copy *A Child's Copybook Reader, Volume 1*, page 22. When he has finished the copywork, invite him to spell any word he remembers. Ask him to spell *sunset*. Encourage him to think of the two shorter words that are put together to form *sunset*; if he is unsure, allow him to look at the word.

Track B: Have your student read aloud *New Friends*, pages 84–88, "Whistle, the Baltimore Oriole."

Math: Work on your selected math curriculum for 15–20 minutes.

Notes

Lesson 24

Materials Needed
- *A Child's Copybook Reader, Volume 1* (Track A)
- *Print to Cursive Proverbs* (Track B)
- SCM science course of choice
- Math course of choice

Track A: Have your student carefully copy *A Child's Copybook Reader, Volume 1*, page 23. When he has finished the copywork, invite him to spell any word he remembers. Ask him to spell *up*; if he is unsure, allow him to look at the word.

Track B: Have your student read aloud the proverb at the top of *Print to Cursive Proverbs*, page 21, then complete the page.

Science: In your SCM science course, complete the second assignment for Week 5.

Math: Work on your selected math curriculum for 15–20 minutes.

Lesson 25

Materials Needed
- Math course of choice
- *Busy Times* (Track A)
- *Print to Cursive Proverbs* (Track B)
- *Journaling a Year in Nature* notebooks (optional)

Math: Work on your selected math curriculum for 15–20 minutes.

Track A: Help your student read aloud *Busy Times*, pages 44–52, "The Goat Cart."

Tip: Don't worry if your student doesn't get through all of pages 44–52. There is a scheduled catch-up time in lesson 27.

Track B: Have your student complete *Print to Cursive Proverbs*, page 22.

Nature Study: Take the whole family outside for nature study.

Lesson 26

Materials Needed
- *A Child's Copybook Reader, Volume 1* (Track A)
- *New Friends* (Track B)
- Math course of choice

Track A: Help your student read aloud *A Child's Copybook Reader, Volume 1*, page 24.

Track B: Have your student read aloud *New Friends*, pages 89–93, "A Family of Pelicans."

Math: Work on your selected math curriculum for 15–20 minutes.

Lesson 27

Materials Needed
- *A Child's Copybook Reader, Volume 1* (Track A)
- *Busy Times*, if needed (Track A)
- *Print to Cursive Proverbs* (Track B)
- Math course of choice
- SCM science course of choice

Track A: Help your student finish reading aloud *Busy Times*, pages 44–52, "The Goat Cart," if needed.

Have your student carefully copy *A Child's Copybook Reader, Volume 1*, page 25. When he has finished the copywork, invite him to spell any word he remembers. Ask him to spell *winter*; if he is unsure, allow him to look at the word.

Track B: Have your student read aloud the proverb in *Print to Cursive Proverbs*, page 23, then carefully copy it. When he has finished the copywork, invite him to spell any word he remembers. Ask him to spell *wise*; if he is unsure, allow him to look at the word.

Math: Work on your selected math curriculum for 15–20 minutes.

Science: In your SCM science course, complete the first assignment for Week 6.

Lesson 28

Materials Needed
- *A Child's Copybook Reader, Volume 1* (Track A)
- *New Friends*, if needed (Track B)
- Math course of choice

Track A: Have your student carefully copy *A Child's Copybook Reader, Volume 1*, page 26. When he has finished the copywork, invite him to spell any word he remembers. Ask him to spell *summer*; if he is unsure, allow him to look at the word.

Track B: Use today to catch up on any assigned reading in *New Friends*, as needed.

Math: Work on your selected math curriculum for 15–20 minutes.

Lesson 29

Materials Needed
- *A Child's Copybook Reader, Volume 1* (Track A)
- *Print to Cursive Proverbs* (Track B)
- SCM science course of choice
- Math course of choice

Track A: Have your student carefully copy *A Child's Copybook Reader, Volume 1*, page 27. When he has finished the copywork, invite him to spell any word he remembers. Ask him to spell *garden*; if he is unsure, allow him to look at the word.

Track B: Have your student read aloud the proverb at the top of *Print to Cursive Proverbs*, page 24, then complete the page.

Science: In your SCM science course, complete the second assignment for Week 6.

Math: Work on your selected math curriculum for 15–20 minutes.

Lesson 30

Materials Needed
- Math course of choice
- *Busy Times* (Track A)
- *Print to Cursive Proverbs* (Track B)
- *Journaling a Year in Nature* notebooks (optional)

Math: Work on your selected math curriculum for 15–20 minutes.

Track A: Help your student read aloud *Busy Times*, pages 53–61, "Whiskers and the Cart."

Tip: Don't worry if your student doesn't get through all of pages 53–61. There is a scheduled catch-up time in lesson 33.

Track B: Have your student complete *Print to Cursive Proverbs*, page 25.

Nature Study: Take the whole family outside for nature study.

Lesson 31

Materials Needed
- *A Child's Copybook Reader, Volume 1* (Track A)
- *New Friends* (Track B)
- Math course of choice

Track A: Have your student carefully copy *A Child's Copybook Reader, Volume 1,* page 28. When he has finished the copywork, invite him to spell any word he remembers. Ask him to spell *one*; if he is unsure, allow him to look at the word.

Track B: Have your student read aloud *New Friends*, pages 98–106, "Great Plans."

Math: Work on your selected math curriculum for 15–20 minutes.

Lesson 32

Materials Needed
- *A Child's Copybook Reader, Volume 1* (Track A)
- *Print to Cursive Proverbs* (Track B)
- Math course of choice
- SCM science course of choice

Track A: Help your student read aloud *A Child's Copybook Reader, Volume 1,* page 29.

Track B: Have your student read aloud the proverb in *Print to Cursive Proverbs,* pages 26 and 27, then carefully copy it. When he has finished the copywork, invite him to spell any word he remembers. Ask him to spell *false*; if he is unsure, allow him to look at the word.

Math: Work on your selected math curriculum for 15–20 minutes.

Science: In your SCM science course, complete the first assignment for Week 7.

Lesson 33

Materials Needed
- *A Child's Copybook Reader, Volume 1* (Track A)
- *Busy Times*, if needed (Track A)
- *New Friends* (Track B)
- Math course of choice

Track A: Help your student finish reading aloud *Busy Times*, pages 53–61, "Whiskers and the Cart," if needed.

Have your student carefully copy *A Child's Copybook Reader, Volume 1,* page 30. When he has finished the copywork, invite him to spell any word he remembers. Ask him to spell *trees*; if he is unsure, allow him to look at the word.

Track B: Have your student read aloud *New Friends*, pages 106–117, "The Surprise Cake."

Math: Work on your selected math curriculum for 15–20 minutes.

Lesson 34

Materials Needed
- *A Child's Copybook Reader, Volume 1* (Track A)
- *Print to Cursive Proverbs* (Track B)
- SCM science course of choice
- Math course of choice

Track A: Have your student carefully copy *A Child's Copybook Reader, Volume 1*, page 31. When he has finished the copywork, invite him to spell any word he remembers. Ask him to spell *we*; if he is unsure, allow him to look at the word.

Track B: Have your student read aloud the proverb at the top of *Print to Cursive Proverbs,* page 28, then complete the page.

Science: In your SCM science course, complete the second assignment for Week 7.

Math: Work on your selected math curriculum for 15–20 minutes.

Lesson 35

Materials Needed
- Math course of choice
- *Busy Times* (Track A)
- *Print to Cursive Proverbs* (Track B)
- *Journaling a Year in Nature* notebooks (optional)

Math: Work on your selected math curriculum for 15–20 minutes.

Track A: Help your student read aloud *Busy Times*, pages 62–72, "Peter Forgets."

Tip: Don't worry if your student doesn't get through all of pages 62–72. There is a scheduled catch-up time in lesson 37.

Track B: Have your student complete *Print to Cursive Proverbs*, page 29.

Nature Study: Take the whole family outside for nature study.

Lesson 36

Materials Needed
- *A Child's Copybook Reader, Volume 1* (Track A)
- *New Friends* (Track B)
- Math course of choice

Track A: Have your student carefully copy *A Child's Copybook Reader, Volume*

1, page 32. When he has finished the copywork, invite him to spell any word he remembers. Ask him to spell *water*; if he is unsure, allow him to look at the word.

Track B: Have your student read aloud *New Friends*, pages 118–127, "Greener Grass."

Math: Work on your selected math curriculum for 15–20 minutes.

Lesson 37

Materials Needed
- *A Child's Copybook Reader, Volume 1* (Track A)
- *Busy Times,* if needed (Track A)
- *Print to Cursive Proverbs* (Track B)
- Math course of choice
- SCM science course of choice

Track A: Help your student finish reading aloud *Busy Times*, pages 62–72, "Peter Forgets," if needed.

Have your student carefully copy *A Child's Copybook Reader, Volume 1,* page 33. When he has finished the copywork, invite him to spell any word he remembers. Ask him to spell *day*; if he is unsure, allow him to look at the word.

Track B: Have your student read aloud the proverb in *Print to Cursive Proverbs,* pages 30 and 31, then carefully copy it. When he has finished the copywork, invite him to spell any word he remembers. Ask him to spell *every*; if he is unsure, allow him to look at the word.

Math: Work on your selected math curriculum for 15–20 minutes.

Science: In your SCM science course, complete the first assignment for Week 8.

Lesson 38

Materials Needed
- *A Child's Copybook Reader, Volume 1* (Track A)
- *New Friends* (Track B)
- Math course of choice

Track A: Help your student read aloud *A Child's Copybook Reader, Volume 1,* page 34.

Track B: Have your student read aloud *New Friends*, pages 127–137, "Work Before Play."

Math: Work on your selected math curriculum for 15–20 minutes.

Lesson 39

Materials Needed
- *A Child's Copybook Reader, Volume 1* (Track A)
- *Print to Cursive Proverbs* (Track B)
- SCM science course of choice
- Math course of choice

Track A: Have your student carefully copy *A Child's Copybook Reader, Volume 1*, page 35. When he has finished the copywork, invite him to spell any word he remembers. Ask him to spell *see*; if he is unsure, allow him to look at the word.

Track B: Have your student read aloud the proverb at the top of *Print to Cursive Proverbs*, page 32, then complete the page.

Science: In your SCM science course, complete the second assignment for Week 8.

Math: Work on your selected math curriculum for 15–20 minutes.

Lesson 40

Materials Needed
- Math course of choice
- *Busy Times* (Track A)
- *Print to Cursive Proverbs* (Track B)
- *Journaling a Year in Nature* notebooks (optional)

Math: Work on your selected math curriculum for 15–20 minutes.

Track A: Help your student read aloud *Busy Times*, pages 73–82, "Good-by, Goat Cart."

Tip: Don't worry if your student doesn't get through all of pages 73–82. There is a scheduled catch-up time in lesson 42.

Track B: Have your student complete *Print to Cursive Proverbs*, page 33.

Nature Study: Take the whole family outside for nature study.

Lesson 41

Materials Needed
- *A Child's Copybook Reader, Volume 1* (Track A)
- *New Friends* (Track B)
- Math course of choice

Track A: Have your student carefully copy *A Child's Copybook Reader, Volume 1*, page 36. When he has finished the copywork, invite him to spell any word he remembers. Ask him to spell *tell*; if he is unsure, allow him to look at the word.

Track B: Have your student read aloud *New Friends*, pages 138–148, "Ten Thousand Babies."

Math: Work on your selected math curriculum for 15–20 minutes.

Lesson 42

Materials Needed
- *A Child's Copybook Reader, Volume 1* (Track A)
- *Busy Times*, if needed (Track A)
- *Print to Cursive Proverbs* (Track B)
- Math course of choice
- SCM science course of choice

Track A: Help your student finish reading aloud *Busy Times*, pages 73–82, "Good-by, Goat Cart," if needed.

Have your student carefully copy *A Child's Copybook Reader, Volume 1*, page 37. When he has finished the copywork, invite him to spell any word he remembers. Ask him to spell *is*; if he is unsure, allow him to look at the word.

Track B: Have your student read aloud the proverb in *Print to Cursive Proverbs*, pages 34 and 35, then carefully copy it. When he has finished the copywork, invite him to spell any word he remembers. Ask him to spell *great*; if he is unsure, allow him to look at the word.

Math: Work on your selected math curriculum for 15–20 minutes.

Science: In your SCM science course, complete the first assignment for Week 9.

Lesson 43

Materials Needed
- *A Child's Copybook Reader, Volume 1* (Track A)
- *New Friends*, if needed (Track B)
- Math course of choice

Track A: Have your student carefully copy *A Child's Copybook Reader, Volume 1*, page 38. When he has finished the copywork, invite him to spell any word he remembers. Ask him to spell *has*; if he is unsure, allow him to look at the word. See if he can also spell *had*.

Track B: Use today to catch up on any assigned reading in *New Friends*, as needed.

Math: Work on your selected math curriculum for 15–20 minutes.

Lesson 44

Materials Needed
- *A Child's Copybook Reader, Volume 1* (Track A)
- *Print to Cursive Proverbs* (Track B)
- SCM science course of choice
- Math course of choice

Track A: Help your student read aloud the entire poem, "All Things Bright and Beautiful," in *A Child's Copybook Reader, Volume 1*, page 39. If desired, review 6–10 of these words and his selected words from previous copywork lessons: *the, running, sunset, up, winter, summer, garden, one, trees, we, water, day, see, tell, is, has, had.* If your student is unsure about a particular word's spelling, allow him to look at the word.

Track B: Have your student read aloud the proverb at the top of *Print to Cursive Proverbs,* page 36, then complete the page.

Science: In your SCM science course, complete the second assignment for Week 9.

Math: Work on your selected math curriculum for 15–20 minutes.

Lesson 45

Materials Needed
- Math course of choice
- *Busy Times* (Track A)
- *Print to Cursive Proverbs* (Track B)
- *Journaling a Year in Nature* notebooks (optional)

Math: Work on your selected math curriculum for 15–20 minutes.

Track A: Help your student read aloud *Busy Times*, pages 84–92, "New Work for Peter."

Tip: Don't worry if your student doesn't get through all of pages 84–92. There is a scheduled catch-up time in lesson 47.

Track B: Have your student complete *Print to Cursive Proverbs,* page 37.

Nature Study: Take the whole family outside for nature study.

Lesson 46

Materials Needed
- *A Child's Copybook Reader, Volume 1* (Track A)

- *New Friends* (Track B)
- Math course of choice

Track A: Help your student read aloud *A Child's Copybook Reader, Volume 1*, page 41.

Track B: Have your student read aloud *New Friends*, pages 152–158, "A Dollar to Spend."

Math: Work on your selected math curriculum for 15–20 minutes.

Lesson 47

Materials Needed
- *A Child's Copybook Reader, Volume 1* (Track A)
- *Busy Times*, if needed (Track A)
- *Print to Cursive Proverbs* (Track B)
- Math course of choice
- SCM science course of choice

Track A: Help your student finish reading aloud *Busy Times*, pages 84–92, "New Work for Peter," if needed.

Have your student carefully copy the first sentence of the fable in *A Child's Copybook Reader, Volume 1*, page 42: "Two frogs lived together in a marsh." When he has finished the copywork, invite him to spell any word he remembers. Ask him to spell *two*; if he is unsure, allow him to look at the word.

Track B: Have your student read aloud the proverb in *Print to Cursive Proverbs*, pages 38 and 39, then carefully copy it. When he has finished the copywork, invite him to spell any word he remembers. Ask him to spell *where*; if he is unsure, allow him to look at the word. Also see if he can spell *there*.

Math: Work on your selected math curriculum for 15–20 minutes.

Science: In your SCM science course, complete the first assignment for Week 10.

Lesson 48

Materials Needed
- *A Child's Copybook Reader, Volume 1* (Track A)
- *New Friends* (Track B)
- Math course of choice

Track A: Have your student carefully copy the next phrase of the fable in *A Child's Copybook Reader, Volume 1*, beginning on page 43: "But one hot summer the marsh dried up,". When he has finished the copywork, invite him to spell any word he remembers. Ask him to spell *but*; if he is unsure, allow him to look at the word.

Track B: Have your student read aloud *New Friends*, pages 159–171, "The Dumbest Thing."

Math: Work on your selected math curriculum for 15–20 minutes.

Lesson 49

Materials Needed
- *A Child's Copybook Reader, Volume 1* (Track A)
- *Print to Cursive Proverbs* (Track B)
- SCM science course of choice
- Math course of choice

Track A: Have your student carefully copy the next phrase of the fable in *A Child's Copybook Reader, Volume 1*, beginning on page 44: "and they left it to look for another place to live in,". When he has finished the copywork, invite him to spell any word he remembers. Ask him to spell *look*; if he is unsure, allow him to look at the word.

Track B: Have your student read aloud the proverb at the top of *Print to Cursive Proverbs*, page 40, then complete the page.

Science: In your SCM science course, complete the second assignment for Week 10.

Math: Work on your selected math curriculum for 15–20 minutes.

Lesson 50

Materials Needed
- Math course of choice
- *Busy Times* (Track A)
- *Print to Cursive Proverbs* (Track B)
- *Journaling a Year in Nature* notebooks (optional)

Math: Work on your selected math curriculum for 15–20 minutes.

Track A: Help your student read aloud *Busy Times*, pages 93–98, "The Golden Rule."

Tip: Don't worry if your student doesn't get through all of pages 93–98. There is a scheduled catch-up time in lesson 53.

Track B: Have your student complete *Print to Cursive Proverbs*, page 41.

Nature Study: Take the whole family outside for nature study.

Lesson 51

Materials Needed
- *A Child's Copybook Reader, Volume 1* (Track A)
- *New Friends* (Track B)
- Math course of choice

Track A: Have your student carefully copy the rest of the sentence in *A Child's Copybook Reader, Volume 1,* beginning on page 45: "for frogs like damp places if they can get them." When he has finished the copywork, invite him to spell any word he remembers. Ask him to spell *get*; if he is unsure, allow him to look at the word.

Track B: Have your student read aloud *New Friends,* pages 171–181, "Mrs. Wright's Gift."

Math: Work on your selected math curriculum for 15–20 minutes.

Lesson 52

Materials Needed
- *A Child's Copybook Reader, Volume 1* (Track A)
- *Print to Cursive Proverbs* (Track B)
- Math course of choice
- SCM science course of choice

Track A: Help your student read aloud *A Child's Copybook Reader, Volume 1,* page 47.

Track B: Have your student read aloud the proverb in *Print to Cursive Proverbs,* pages 42 and 43, then carefully copy it. When he has finished the copywork, invite him to spell any word he remembers. Ask him to spell *green*; if he is unsure, allow him to look at the word.

Math: Work on your selected math curriculum for 15–20 minutes.

Science: In your SCM science course, complete the first assignment for Week 11.

Lesson 53

Materials Needed
- *A Child's Copybook Reader, Volume 1* (Track A)
- *Busy Times,* if needed (Track A)
- *New Friends* (Track A)
- Math course of choice

Track A: Help your student finish reading aloud *Busy Times,* pages 93–98, "The Golden Rule," if needed.

Notes

Have your student carefully copy the phrase of the fable in *A Child's Copybook Reader, Volume 1,* on page 48: "By and by they came to a deep well,". When he has finished the copywork, invite him to spell any word he remembers. Ask him to spell *by;* if he is unsure, allow him to look at the word.

Track B: Have your student read aloud *New Friends,* pages 182–194, "A Fitting Name."

Math: Work on your selected math curriculum for 15–20 minutes.

Lesson 54

Materials Needed
- *A Child's Copybook Reader, Volume 1* (Track A)
- *Print to Cursive Proverbs* (Track B)
- SCM science course of choice
- Math course of choice

Track A: Have your student carefully copy the next phrase of the fable in *A Child's Copybook Reader, Volume 1,* on page 49: "and one of them looked down into it". When he has finished the copywork, invite him to spell any word he remembers. Ask him to spell *down;* if he is unsure, allow him to look at the word.

Track B: Have your student read aloud the proverb at the top of *Print to Cursive Proverbs,* page 44, then complete the page.

Science: In your SCM science course, complete the second assignment for Week 11.

Math: Work on your selected math curriculum for 15–20 minutes.

Lesson 55

Materials Needed
- Math course of choice
- *Busy Times* (Track A)
- *Print to Cursive Proverbs* (Track B)
- *Journaling a Year in Nature* notebooks (optional)

Math: Work on your selected math curriculum for 15–20 minutes.

Track A: Help your student read aloud *Busy Times,* pages 99–105, "Rachel's Candy."

Tip: Don't worry if your student doesn't get through all of pages 99–105. There is a scheduled catch-up time in lesson 57.

Track B: Have your student complete *Print to Cursive Proverbs*, page 45.

Nature Study: Take the whole family outside for nature study.

Lesson 56

Materials Needed
- *A Child's Copybook Reader, Volume 1* (Track A)
- *New Friends* (Track B)
- Math course of choice

Track A: Have your student carefully copy the rest of the sentence in *A Child's Copybook Reader, Volume 1,* beginning on page 50: "and said to the other, 'This looks like a nice cool place." When he has finished the copywork, invite him to spell any word he remembers. Ask him to spell *this*; if he is unsure, allow him to look at the word.

Tip: Point out the beginning quotation marks that signify what the frog said. The student will not put the ending quotation marks in place until he copies the rest of the frog's remark tomorrow.

Track B: Have your student read aloud *New Friends*, pages 194–204, "The Missing Cow."

Math: Work on your selected math curriculum for 15–20 minutes.

Lesson 57

Materials Needed
- *A Child's Copybook Reader, Volume 1* (Track A)
- *Busy Times,* if needed (Track A)
- *Print to Cursive Proverbs* (Track B)
- Math course of choice
- SCM science course of choice

Track A: Help your student finish reading aloud *Busy Times*, pages 99–105, "Rachel's Candy," if needed.

Have your student carefully copy the next sentence of the fable in *A Child's Copybook Reader, Volume 1,* beginning on page 51: "Let us jump in and settle here." When he has finished the copywork, invite him to spell any word he remembers. Ask him to spell *let*; if he is unsure, allow him to look at the word.

Track B: Have your student read aloud the proverb in *Print to Cursive Proverbs,* page 46, then carefully copy it. When he has finished the copywork, invite him to spell any word he remembers. Ask him to spell *just*; if he is unsure, allow him to look at the word.

Notes

Math: Work on your selected math curriculum for 15–20 minutes.

Science: In your SCM science course, complete the first assignment for Week 12.

Reminder: Get A Child's Copybook Reader, Volume 2, *for Track A for lesson 67.*

Lesson 58

Materials Needed
- *A Child's Copybook Reader, Volume 1,* if needed (Track A)
- *New Friends* (Track B)
- Math course of choice

Track A: Use today to catch up on any assigned copywork in *A Child's Copybook Reader, Volume 1,* as needed.

Track B: Have your student read aloud *New Friends,* pages 204–215, "Better Than Ice Cream."

Math: Work on your selected math curriculum for 15–20 minutes.

Lesson 59

Materials Needed
- *A Child's Copybook Reader, Volume 1* (Track A)
- *Print to Cursive Proverbs,* if needed (Track B)
- SCM science course of choice
- Math course of choice

Track A: Help your student read aloud *A Child's Copybook Reader, Volume 1,* page 53.

Track B: Use today and tomorrow to catch up on any assigned pages in *Print to Cursive Proverbs,* as needed. If desired, review these words and some of your student's selected words from previous copywork lessons: *turns, wise, false, every.* If your student is unsure about a particular word's spelling, allow him to look at the word.

Science: In your SCM science course, complete the second assignment for Week 12.

Math: Work on your selected math curriculum for 15–20 minutes.

Lesson 60

Materials Needed

- Math course of choice
- *Busy Times* (Track A)
- *Print to Cursive Proverbs*, if needed (Track B)
- *Journaling a Year in Nature* notebooks (optional)

Math: Work on your selected math curriculum for 15–20 minutes.

Track A: Help your student read aloud *Busy Times*, pages 106–118, "Andrew and the Cats."

Tip: From this point on, the scheduled catch-up lessons for readings in Busy Times *will be less frequent. If you need more than one lesson time to read through a chapter, simply begin where you left off instead of starting a new chapter at each lesson. The important thing is to go at your student's pace and not frustrate him.*

Track B: Use today to catch up on any assigned pages in *Print to Cursive Proverbs,* as needed. If desired, review these words and more of your student's selected words from previous copywork lessons: *great, where, there, green, just.* If your student is unsure about a particular word's spelling, allow him to look at the word.

Nature Study: Take the whole family outside for nature study.

Term 2

(12 weeks; 5 lessons/week)

Term 2 Resources List
- Math course of choice
- Simply Charlotte Mason (SCM) science course of choice
- *Journaling a Year in Nature* notebooks (optional)

Track A
- *A Child's Copybook Reader, Volumes 1 and 2*
- *Busy Times*
- *More Busy Times*

Track B
- *Print to Cursive Proverbs*
- *New Friends*
- *More New Friends*

Weekly Schedule

	Day One	Day Two	Day Three	Day Four	Day Five
	Math (15–20 min.)	Math (15–20 min.)	Math (15–20 min.)	Math (15–20 min.)	Math (15–20 min.)
	(Nature Study)		Science (15–20 min.)		Science (15–20 min.)
Track A	Copybook Reader (5 min.)	Copybook Reader (5 min.); Busy Times (10–15 min.)	Copybook Reader (5 min.)	Copybook Reader (5 min.)	Busy Times (10–15 min.)
Track B	New Friends (10–15 min.)	Print to Cursive Proverbs (5–10 min.)	Print to Cursive Proverbs (5–10 min.)	New Friends (10–15 min.)	Print to Cursive Proverbs (5–10 min.)

Lesson 61

Materials Needed
- *A Child's Copybook Reader, Volume 1* (Track A)
- *New Friends,* if needed (Track B)
- Math course of choice
- *Journaling a Year in Nature* notebooks (optional)

Track A: Have your student carefully copy the next phrase of the fable in *A Child's Copybook Reader, Volume 1*, beginning on page 54: "But the other, who had a wiser head on his shoulders,". When he has finished the copywork, invite him to spell any word he remembers. Ask him to spell *other*; if he is unsure, allow him to look at the word.

Track B: Use today to catch up on any assigned reading in *New Friends*, as needed.

Math: Work on your selected math curriculum for 15–20 minutes.

Nature Study: Take the whole family outside for nature study.

Lesson 62

Materials Needed
- Math course of choice
- *A Child's Copybook Reader, Volume 1* (Track A)
- *Busy Times* (Track A)
- *Print to Cursive Proverbs* (Track B)

Math: Work on your selected math curriculum for 15–20 minutes.

Track A: Have your student carefully copy the next phrase of the fable in *A Child's Copybook Reader, Volume 1*, beginning on page 55: "replied, 'Not so fast, my friend. If this well dried up." When he has finished the copywork, invite him to spell any word he remembers. Ask him to spell *my*; if he is unsure, allow him to look at the word.

Help your student read aloud *Busy Times*, pages 119–128, "The Working Bee."

Track B: Have your student read aloud the proverb at the top of *Print to Cursive Proverbs*, page 47, then complete the page.

Lesson 63

Materials Needed
- *A Child's Copybook Reader, Volume 1* (Track A)
- *Print to Cursive Proverbs* (Track B)
- Math course of choice
- SCM science course of choice

Notes

Track A: Have your student carefully copy the rest of the sentence in *A Child's Copybook Reader, Volume 1,* beginning on page 57: "like the marsh, how should we get out again?" When he has finished the copywork, invite him to spell any word he remembers. Ask him to spell *out*; if he is unsure, allow him to look at the word.

Track B: Have your student complete *Print to Cursive Proverbs*, page 48.

Math: Work on your selected math curriculum for 15–20 minutes.

Science: In your SCM science course, complete the first assignment for Week 13.

Lesson 64

Materials Needed
- *A Child's Copybook Reader, Volume 1* (Track A)
- *New Friends* (Track B)
- Math course of choice

Track A: Have your student carefully copy the moral of the fable in *A Child's Copybook Reader, Volume 1,* beginning on page 58: "Moral: Think twice before you act." When he has finished the copywork, invite him to spell any word he remembers. Ask him to spell *think*; if he is unsure, allow him to look at the word.

Track B: Have your student read aloud *New Friends*, pages 218–228, "Report Cards."

Math: Work on your selected math curriculum for 15–20 minutes.

Lesson 65

Materials Needed
- *Busy Times* (Track A)
- *Print to Cursive Proverbs* (Track B)
- Math course of choice
- SCM science course of choice

Track A: Help your student read aloud *Busy Times,* pages 130–137, "The Only Girl."

Track B: Have your student read aloud the proverb in *Print to Cursive Proverbs,* pages 49 and 50, then carefully copy it. When he has finished the copywork, invite him to spell any word he remembers. Ask him to spell *known*; if he is unsure, allow him to look at the word.

Math: Work on your selected math curriculum for 15–20 minutes.

Science: In your SCM science course, complete the second assignment for Week 13.

Lesson 66

Materials Needed
- *A Child's Copybook Reader, Volume 1* (Track A)
- *New Friends* (Track B)
- Math course of choice
- *Journaling a Year in Nature* notebooks (optional)

Track A: Help your student read the fable in *A Child's Copybook Reader, Volume 1,* page 60. If desired, review 6–10 of these words and his selected words from previous copywork lessons: *two, but, look, get, by, down, this, let, other, my, out, think.* If your student is unsure about a particular word's spelling, allow him to look at the word.

Track B: Have your student read aloud *New Friends,* pages 228–238, "Chore Time."

Math: Work on your selected math curriculum for 15–20 minutes.

Nature Study: Take the whole family outside for nature study.

Lesson 67

Materials Needed
- Math course of choice
- *A Child's Copybook Reader, Volume 2* (Track A)
- *Busy Times,* if needed (Track A)
- *Print to Cursive Proverbs* (Track B)

Math: Work on your selected math curriculum for 15–20 minutes.

Track A: Have your student read aloud the stanza in *A Child's Copybook Reader, Volume 2,* page 4, then carefully copy page 5. When he has finished the copywork, invite him to spell any word he remembers. Ask him to spell *its;* if he is unsure, allow him to look at the word.

Use today to catch up on any assigned reading from *Busy Times,* as needed.

Track B: Have your student read aloud the proverb at the top of *Print to Cursive Proverbs,* page 51, then complete the page.

Lesson 68

Materials Needed
- *A Child's Copybook Reader, Volume 2* (Track A)
- *Print to Cursive Proverbs* (Track B)

- Math course of choice
- SCM science course of choice

Track A: Have your student carefully copy *A Child's Copybook Reader, Volume 2,* page 6. When he has finished the copywork, invite him to spell any word he remembers. Ask him to spell *go*; if he is unsure, allow him to look at the word.

Track B: Have your student complete *Print to Cursive Proverbs,* page 52.

Math: Work on your selected math curriculum for 15–20 minutes.

Science: In your SCM science course, complete the first assignment for Week 14.

Lesson 69

Materials Needed
- *A Child's Copybook Reader, Volume 2* (Track A)
- *New Friends* (Track B)
- Math course of choice

Track A: Have your student read aloud the stanza in *A Child's Copybook Reader, Volume 2,* page 7, then carefully copy page 8. When he has finished the copywork, invite him to spell any word he remembers. Ask him to spell *was*; if he is unsure, allow him to look at the word.

Track B: Have your student read aloud *New Friends*, pages 239–250, "One Part of Life."

Math: Work on your selected math curriculum for 15–20 minutes.

Lesson 70

Materials Needed
- *Busy Times* (Track A)
- *Print to Cursive Proverbs* (Track B)
- Math course of choice
- SCM science course of choice

Track A: Help your student read aloud *Busy Times*, pages 138–143, "Getting Ready to Move."

Track B: Have your student read aloud the proverb in *Print to Cursive Proverbs,* pages 53 and 54, then carefully copy it. When he has finished the copywork, invite him to spell any word he remembers. Ask him to spell *takes*; if he is unsure, allow him to look at the word.

Math: Work on your selected math curriculum for 15–20 minutes.

Science: In your SCM science course, complete the second assignment for Week 14.

Lesson 71

Materials Needed
- *A Child's Copybook Reader, Volume 2* (Track A)
- *New Friends* (Track B)
- Math course of choice
- *Journaling a Year in Nature* notebooks (optional)

Track A: Have your student carefully copy *A Child's Copybook Reader, Volume 2,* page 9. When he has finished the copywork, invite him to spell any word he remembers. Ask him to spell *play*; if he is unsure, allow him to look at the word.

Track B: Have your student read aloud *New Friends*, pages 251–261, "A Trick for Dad."

Math: Work on your selected math curriculum for 15–20 minutes.

Nature Study: Take the whole family outside for nature study.

Lesson 72

Materials Needed
- Math course of choice
- *A Child's Copybook Reader, Volume 2* (Track A)
- *Busy Times* (Track A)
- *Print to Cursive Proverbs* (Track B)

Math: Work on your selected math curriculum for 15–20 minutes.

Track A: Have your student read aloud the stanza in *A Child's Copybook Reader, Volume 2*, page 10, then carefully copy page 11. When he has finished the copywork, invite him to spell any word he remembers. Ask him to spell *so*; if he is unsure, allow him to look at the word.
　　Help your student read aloud *Busy Times*, pages 144–154, "A Busy Day."

Track B: Have your student read aloud the proverb at the top of *Print to Cursive Proverbs*, page 55, then complete the page.

Lesson 73

Materials Needed
- *A Child's Copybook Reader, Volume 2* (Track A)
- *Print to Cursive Proverbs* (Track B)
- Math course of choice
- SCM science course of choice

Track A: Have your student carefully copy *A Child's Copybook Reader, Volume 2*, page 12. When he has finished the copywork, invite him to spell any word he remembers. Ask him to spell *about*; if he is unsure, allow him to look at the word.

Track B: Have your student complete *Print to Cursive Proverbs*, page 56.

Math: Work on your selected math curriculum for 15–20 minutes.

Science: In your SCM science course, complete the first assignment for Week 15.

Lesson 74

Materials Needed
- *A Child's Copybook Reader, Volume 2* (Track A)
- *New Friends* (Track B)
- Math course of choice

Track A: Have your student read aloud the stanza in *A Child's Copybook Reader, Volume 2*, page 13, then carefully copy page 14. When he has finished the copywork, invite him to spell any word he remembers. Ask him to spell *her*; if he is unsure, allow him to look at the word.

Track B: Have your student read aloud *New Friends*, pages 261–268, "A Glass of Warm Water."

Math: Work on your selected math curriculum for 15–20 minutes.

Reminder: Get More New Friends *for Track B for lesson 84.*

Lesson 75

Materials Needed
- *Busy Times* (Track A)
- *Print to Cursive Proverbs* (Track B)
- Math course of choice
- SCM science course of choice

Track A: Help your student read aloud *Busy Times,* pages 155–166, "The Long Ride."

Track B: Have your student read aloud the proverb in *Print to Cursive Proverbs*, pages 57 and 58, then carefully copy it. When he has finished the copywork, invite him to spell any word he remembers. Ask him to spell *opens*; if he is unsure, allow him to look at the word.

Math: Work on your selected math curriculum for 15–20 minutes.

Science: In your SCM science course, complete the second assignment for Week 15.

Lesson 76

Materials Needed
- *A Child's Copybook Reader, Volume 2* (Track A)
- *New Friends* (Track B)
- Math course of choice
- *Journaling a Year in Nature* notebooks (optional)

Track A: Have your student carefully copy *A Child's Copybook Reader, Volume 2,* page 15. When he has finished the copywork, invite him to spell any word he remembers. Ask him to spell *said*; if he is unsure, allow him to look at the word.

Track B: Have your student read aloud *New Friends,* pages 268–279, "Bitternut Hickory."

Math: Work on your selected math curriculum for 15–20 minutes.

Nature Study: Take the whole family outside for nature study.

Lesson 77

Materials Needed
- Math course of choice
- *A Child's Copybook Reader, Volume 2* (Track A)
- *Busy Times*, if needed (Track A)
- *Print to Cursive Proverbs* (Track B)

Math: Work on your selected math curriculum for 15–20 minutes.

Track A: Have your student read aloud the stanza in *A Child's Copybook Reader, Volume 2,* page 16, then carefully copy page 17. When he has finished the copywork, invite him to spell any word he remembers. Ask him to spell *love*; if he is unsure, allow him to look at the word.
　　Use today to catch up on any assigned reading from *Busy Times*, as needed.

Track B: Have your student read aloud the proverb at the top of *Print to Cursive Proverbs*, page 59, then complete the page.

Lesson 78

Materials Needed
- *A Child's Copybook Reader, Volume 2* (Track A)
- *Print to Cursive Proverbs* (Track B)

- Math course of choice
- SCM science course of choice

Track A: Have your student carefully copy *A Child's Copybook Reader, Volume 2,* page 18. When he has finished the copywork, invite him to spell any word he remembers. Ask him to spell *did*; if he is unsure, allow him to look at the word.

Track B: Have your student complete *Print to Cursive Proverbs,* page 60.

Math: Work on your selected math curriculum for 15–20 minutes.

Science: In your SCM science course, complete the first assignment for Week 16.

Lesson 79

Materials Needed
- *A Child's Copybook Reader, Volume 2* (Track A)
- *New Friends,* if needed (Track B)
- Math course of choice

Track A: Have your student read aloud the stanza in *A Child's Copybook Reader, Volume 2*, page 19, then carefully copy page 20. When he has finished the copywork, invite him to spell any word he remembers. Ask him to spell *you*; if he is unsure, allow him to look at the word.

Track B: Use today and lesson 81 to catch up on any assigned reading in *New Friends,* as needed.

Math: Work on your selected math curriculum for 15–20 minutes.

Lesson 80

Materials Needed
- *Busy Times* (Track A)
- *Print to Cursive Proverbs,* if needed (Track B)
- Math course of choice
- SCM science course of choice

Track A: Help your student read aloud *Busy Times*, pages 167–179, "The New Farm."

Track B: Use today to catch up on any assigned pages in *Print to Cursive Proverbs*, as needed. If desired, review these words and your student's selected words from previous copywork lessons: *known, takes, opens.* If your student is unsure about a particular word's spelling, allow him to look at the word.

Math: Work on your selected math curriculum for 15–20 minutes.

Science: In your SCM science course, complete the second assignment for Week 16.

Lesson 81

Materials Needed
- *A Child's Copybook Reader, Volume 2* (Track A)
- *New Friends*, if needed (Track B)
- Math course of choice
- *Journaling a Year in Nature* notebooks (optional)

Track A: Have your student carefully copy *A Child's Copybook Reader, Volume 2*, page 21. When he has finished the copywork, invite him to spell any word he remembers. Ask him to spell *make*; if he is unsure, allow him to look at the word. See if he can also spell *call*.

Track B: Use today to catch up on any assigned reading in *New Friends*, as needed.

Math: Work on your selected math curriculum for 15–20 minutes.

Nature Study: Take the whole family outside for nature study.

Lesson 82

Materials Needed
- Math course of choice
- *A Child's Copybook Reader, Volume 2* (Track A)
- *Busy Times* (Track A)
- *Print to Cursive Proverbs* (Track B)

Math: Work on your selected math curriculum for 15–20 minutes.

Track A: Have your student read aloud "Mary's Lamb" from *A Child's Copybook Reader, Volume 2*, page 22. If desired, review 6–10 of these words and his selected words from previous copywork lessons: *its, go, was, play, so, about, her, said, did, you, make, call*. If your student is unsure about a particular word's spelling, allow him to look at the word.

    Help your student read aloud *Busy Times*, pages 180–189, "An Evening with Peter and Rachel."

Track B: Have your student read aloud the proverb in *Print to Cursive Proverbs*, pages 61 and 62, then carefully copy it. When he has finished the copywork, invite him to spell any word he remembers. Ask him to spell *does*; if he is unsure, allow him to look at the word.

Lesson 83

Materials Needed
- *A Child's Copybook Reader, Volume 2* (Track A)
- *Print to Cursive Proverbs* (Track B)
- Math course of choice
- SCM science course of choice

Track A: Have your student read aloud the paragraph in *A Child's Copybook Reader, Volume 2,* page 24.

Track B: Have your student read aloud the proverb at the top of *Print to Cursive Proverbs*, page 63, then complete the page.

Math: Work on your selected math curriculum for 15–20 minutes.

Science: In your SCM science course, complete the first assignment for Week 17.

Lesson 84

Materials Needed
- *A Child's Copybook Reader, Volume 2* (Track A)
- *More New Friends* (Track B)
- Math course of choice

Track A: Have your student carefully copy the first two sentences of the story in *A Child's Copybook Reader, Volume 2*, beginning on page 25: "Hal Smith has a big farm. He has lofts filled with apples and barns filled with barley." When he has finished the copywork, invite him to spell any word he remembers. Ask him to spell *with*; if he is unsure, allow him to look at the word.

Track B: Have your student read aloud *More New Friends,* pages 6–10, "An Exciting Day."

Math: Work on your selected math curriculum for 15–20 minutes.

Lesson 85

Materials Needed
- *Busy Times* (Track A)
- *Print to Cursive Proverbs* (Track B)
- Math course of choice
- SCM science course of choice

Track A: Help your student read aloud *Busy Times*, pages 190–198, "Home at Last."

Track B: Have your student complete *Print to Cursive Proverbs*, page 64.

Math: Work on your selected math curriculum for 15–20 minutes.

Science: In your SCM science course, complete the second assignment for Week 17.

Lesson 86

Materials Needed
- *A Child's Copybook Reader, Volume 2* (Track A)
- *More New Friends* (Track A)
- Math course of choice
- *Journaling a Year in Nature* notebooks (optional)

Track A: Have your student carefully copy the next sentence of the story in *A Child's Copybook Reader, Volume 2*, beginning on page 26: "He has a windmill on the top of the hill and a garden at the bottom of it." When he has finished the copywork, invite him to spell any word he remembers. Ask him to spell *on*; if he is unsure, allow him to look at the word.

Track B: Have your student read aloud *More New Friends*, pages 10–20, "Tusky, An African Elephant."

Math: Work on your selected math curriculum for 15–20 minutes.

Nature Study: Take the whole family outside for nature study.

Lesson 87

Materials Needed
- Math course of choice
- *A Child's Copybook Reader, Volume 2* (Track A)
- *Busy Times*, if needed (Track A)
- *Print to Cursive Proverbs* (Track B)

Math: Work on your selected math curriculum for 15–20 minutes.

Track A: Have your student carefully copy the next sentence of the story in *A Child's Copybook Reader, Volume 2*, beginning on page 27: "In his farmyard he has hens and chickens, cocks and ducks, pigs and dogs." When he has finished the copywork, invite him to spell any word he remembers. Ask him to spell *his*; if he is unsure, allow him to look at the word.

Use today to catch up on any assigned reading in *Busy Times*, as needed.

Track B: Have your student read aloud the proverb in *Print to Cursive Proverbs*, pages 65 and 66, then carefully copy it. When he has finished the copywork, invite him to spell any word he remembers. Ask him to spell *heart*; if he is unsure, allow him to look at the word.

Lesson 88

Materials Needed
- *A Child's Copybook Reader, Volume 2* (Track A)
- *Print to Cursive Proverbs* (Track B)
- Math course of choice
- SCM science course of choice

Track A: Have your student read aloud the paragraph in *A Child's Copybook Reader, Volume 2,* page 29, then carefully copy the first sentence on page 30: "Hal has six boys." When he has finished the copywork, invite him to spell any word he remembers. Ask him to spell *boys*; if he is unsure, allow him to look at the word.

Track B: Have your student read aloud the proverb at the top of *Print to Cursive Proverbs,* page 67, then complete the page.

Math: Work on your selected math curriculum for 15–20 minutes.

Science: In your SCM science course, complete the first assignment for Week 18.

Lesson 89

Materials Needed
- *A Child's Copybook Reader, Volume 2* (Track A)
- *More New Friends* (Track B)
- Math course of choice

Track A: Have your student carefully copy the next sentence of the story in *A Child's Copybook Reader, Volume 2,* beginning on page 30: "They are strong and willing, and help their Daddy as much as they can." When he has finished the copywork, invite him to spell any word he remembers. Ask him to spell *are*; if he is unsure, allow him to look at the word. See if he can also spell *they*.

Track B: Have your student read aloud *More New Friends*, pages 20–32, "King of the Mountain."

Math: Work on your selected math curriculum for 15–20 minutes.

Lesson 90

Materials Needed
- *Busy Times* (Track A)
- *Print to Cursive Proverbs* (Track B)
- Math course of choice
- SCM science course of choice

Track A: Help your student read aloud *Busy Times*, pages 200–209, "We Want a Pony."

Track B: Have your student complete *Print to Cursive Proverbs*, page 68.

Math: Work on your selected math curriculum for 15–20 minutes.

Science: In your SCM science course, complete the second assignment for Week 18.

Lesson 91

Materials Needed
- *A Child's Copybook Reader, Volume 2* (Track A)
- *More New Friends* (Track A)
- Math course of choice
- *Journaling a Year in Nature* notebooks (optional)

Track A: Have your student carefully copy the next sentence of the story in *A Child's Copybook Reader, Volume 2,* beginning on page 31: "Mark is the eldest; he goes with the cart to the mill." When he has finished the copywork, invite him to spell any word he remembers. Ask him to spell *cart*; if he is unsure, allow him to look at the word.

Tip: If desired, point out the semicolon and how it connects two complete sentences.

Track B: Have your student read aloud *More New Friends*, pages 32–42, "Alice, the Alligator."

Math: Work on your selected math curriculum for 15–20 minutes.

Nature Study: Take the whole family outside for nature study.

Lesson 92

Materials Needed
- Math course of choice
- *A Child's Copybook Reader, Volume 2* (Track A)
- *Busy Times* (Track A)
- *Print to Cursive Proverbs* (Track B)

Math: Work on your selected math curriculum for 15–20 minutes.

Track A: Have your student carefully copy the next sentence of the story in *A Child's Copybook Reader, Volume 2,* beginning on page 32: "Timothy is the next; he thrashes the barley in the barn." When he has finished the copywork,

Notes

invite him to spell any word he remembers. Ask him to spell *he*; if he is unsure, allow him to look at the word.

Help your student read aloud *Busy Times,* pages 210–222, "The New Bat."

Track B: Have your student read aloud the proverb in *Print to Cursive Proverbs,* pages 69 and 70, then carefully copy it. When he has finished the copywork, invite him to spell any word he remembers. Ask him to spell *give*; if he is unsure, allow him to look at the word.

Reminder: Get More Busy Times *for Track A for lesson 102.*

Lesson 93

Materials Needed
- *A Child's Copybook Reader, Volume 2* (Track A)
- *Print to Cursive Proverbs* (Track B)
- Math course of choice
- SCM science course of choice

Track A: Have your student read aloud the paragraph in *A Child's Copybook Reader, Volume 2,* page 34, then carefully copy the first sentence, beginning on page 35: "Martin is the next; he goes to market to sell the eggs and milk." When he has finished the copywork, invite him to spell any word he remembers. Ask him to spell *to*; if he is unsure, allow him to look at the word.

Track B: Have your student read aloud the proverb at the top of *Print to Cursive Proverbs,* page 71, then complete the page.

Math: Work on your selected math curriculum for 15–20 minutes.

Science: In your SCM science course, complete the first assignment for Week 19.

Lesson 94

Materials Needed
- *A Child's Copybook Reader, Volume 2* (Track A)
- *More New Friends* (Track B)
- Math course of choice

Track A: Have your student carefully copy the next sentence of the story in *A Child's Copybook Reader, Volume 2,* on page 36: "Bill is the next; he digs in the garden." When he has finished the copywork, invite him to spell any word he remembers. Ask him to spell *digs*; if he is unsure, allow him to look at the word.

Track B: Have your student read aloud *More New Friends,* pages 42–50, "Shaggy, the Buffalo."

Math: Work on your selected math curriculum for 15–20 minutes.

Lesson 95

Materials Needed
- *Busy Times* (Track A)
- *Print to Cursive Proverbs* (Track B)
- Math course of choice
- SCM science course of choice

Track A: Help your student read aloud *Busy Times*, pages 223–232, "Who Broke the Bat?"

Track B: Have your student complete *Print to Cursive Proverbs*, page 72.

Math: Work on your selected math curriculum for 15–20 minutes.

Science: In your SCM science course, complete the second assignment for Week 19.

Lesson 96

Materials Needed
- *A Child's Copybook Reader, Volume 2* (Track A)
- *More New Friends,* if needed (Track B)
- Math course of choice
- *Journaling a Year in Nature* notebooks (optional)

Track A: Have your student carefully copy the next sentence of the story in *A Child's Copybook Reader, Volume 1,* beginning on page 36: "Charley is the next; he gives the pigs their slop, and the chickens their crumbs." When he has finished the copywork, invite him to spell any word he remembers. Ask him to spell *pigs*; if he is unsure, allow him to look at the word.

Track B: Use today to catch up on any assigned reading in *More New Friends,* as needed.

Math: Work on your selected math curriculum for 15–20 minutes.

Nature Study: Take the whole family outside for nature study.

Lesson 97

Materials Needed
- Math course of choice
- *A Child's Copybook Reader, Volume 2* (Track A)
- *Busy Times* (Track A)
- *Print to Cursive Proverbs,* if needed (Track B)

Math: Work on your selected math curriculum for 15–20 minutes.

Track A: Have your student carefully copy the next sentence of the story in *A Child's Copybook Reader, Volume 2,* on page 38: "Josh is the last." When he has finished the copywork, invite him to spell any word he remembers. Ask him to spell *last;* if he is unsure, allow him to look at the word.

Help your student read aloud *Busy Times,* pages 233–245, "Nancy Makes Things Right."

Track B: Use today to catch up on any assigned pages in *Print to Cursive Proverbs,* as needed. If desired, review these words and your student's selected words from previous copywork lessons: *does, heart, give.* If your student is unsure about a particular word's spelling, allow him to look at the word.

Lesson 98

Materials Needed
- *A Child's Copybook Reader, Volume 2* (Track A)
- *Print to Cursive Proverbs* (Track B)
- Math course of choice
- SCM science course of choice

Track A: Have your student carefully copy the last sentence of the story in *A Child's Copybook Reader, Volume 2,* beginning on page 38: "He is so little that he cannot do much yet, but he runs on errands very willingly." When he has finished the copywork, invite him to spell any word he remembers. Ask him to spell *do;* if he is unsure, allow him to look at the word. See if he can also spell *much.*

Track B: Have your student read aloud the proverb in *Print to Cursive Proverbs,* pages 73 and 74, then carefully copy it. When he has finished the copywork, invite him to spell any word he remembers. Ask him to spell *water;* if he is unsure, allow him to look at the word.

Math: Work on your selected math curriculum for 15–20 minutes.

Science: In your SCM science course, complete the first assignment for Week 20.

Lesson 99

Materials Needed
- *A Child's Copybook Reader, Volume 2* (Track A)
- *More New Friends* (Track B)
- Math course of choice

Track A: Have your student read aloud the story in *A Child's Copybook Reader, Volume 2,* on page 40. If desired, review 6–10 of these words and his selected words from previous copywork lessons: *with, on, his, boys, they, are, cart, he,* *to, digs, pigs, last, do, much.* If your student is unsure about a particular word's spelling, allow him to look at the word.

Track B: Have your student read aloud *More New Friends,* pages 52–64, "The Snaky Bridge."

Math: Work on your selected math curriculum for 15–20 minutes.

Lesson 100

Materials Needed
- *Busy Times,* if needed (Track A)
- *Print to Cursive Proverbs* (Track B)
- Math course of choice
- SCM science course of choice

Track A: Use today to catch up on any assigned reading in *Busy Times,* as needed.

Track B: Have your student read aloud the proverb at the top of *Print to Cursive Proverbs,* page 75, then complete the page.

Math: Work on your selected math curriculum for 15–20 minutes.

Science: In your SCM science course, complete the second assignment for Week 20.

Lesson 101

Materials Needed
- *A Child's Copybook Reader, Volume 2* (Track A)
- *More New Friends* (Track B)
- Math course of choice
- *Journaling a Year in Nature* notebooks (optional)

Track A: Have your student read aloud *A Child's Copybook Reader, Volume 2,* page 42.

Track B: Have your student read aloud *More New Friends,* pages 64–76, "Crossing the Bridge."

Math: Work on your selected math curriculum for 15–20 minutes.

Nature Study: Take the whole family outside for nature study.

Lesson 102

Materials Needed
- Math course of choice

- *A Child's Copybook Reader, Volume 2* (Track A)
- *More Busy Times* (Track A)
- *Print to Cursive Proverbs* (Track B)

Math: Work on your selected math curriculum for 15–20 minutes.

Track A: Have your student carefully copy the first part of the Scripture passage in *A Child's Copybook Reader, Volume 2,* page 43: "Everyone then who hears these words of mine and does them." When he has finished the copywork, invite him to spell any word he remembers. Ask him to spell *then*; if he is unsure, allow him to look at the word.

Help your student read aloud *More Busy Times,* pages 6–15, "What's Wrong with Rachel?"

Track B: Have your student complete *Print to Cursive Proverbs,* page 76. When he has finished the copywork, invite him to spell any word he remembers. Ask him to spell *quick*; if he is unsure, allow him to look at the word.

Lesson 103

Materials Needed
- *A Child's Copybook Reader, Volume 2* (Track A)
- *Print to Cursive Proverbs* (Track B)
- Math course of choice
- SCM science course of choice

Track A: Have your student carefully copy the rest of the sentence in *A Child's Copybook Reader, Volume 2*, on page 44: "will be like a wise man who built his house on the rock." When he has finished the copywork, invite him to spell any word he remembers. Ask him to spell *who*; if he is unsure, allow him to look at the word.

Track B: Have your student read aloud the proverb at the top of *Print to Cursive Proverbs*, page 77, then complete pages 77 and 78.

Math: Work on your selected math curriculum for 15–20 minutes.

Science: In your SCM science course, complete the first assignment for Week 21.

Lesson 104

Materials Needed
- *A Child's Copybook Reader, Volume 2* (Track A)
- *More New Friends* (Track B)
- Math course of choice

Track A: Have your student carefully copy the first part of the next sentence of the Scripture passage in *A Child's Copybook Reader, Volume 2,* beginning on page 45: "And the rain fell, and the floods came, and the winds blew and beat on that house,". When he has finished the copywork, invite him to spell any word he remembers. Ask him to spell *rain*; if he is unsure, allow him to look at the word.

Track B: Have your student read aloud *More New Friends,* pages 77–88, "Busy Days."

Math: Work on your selected math curriculum for 15–20 minutes.

Lesson 105

Materials Needed
- *More Busy Times* (Track A)
- *Print to Cursive Proverbs* (Track B)
- Math course of choice
- SCM science course of choice

Track A: Help your student read aloud *More Busy Times*, pages 16–26, "Peter's Plan."

Track B: Have your student complete *Print to Cursive Proverbs*, page 79. When he has finished the copywork, invite him to spell any word he remembers. Ask him to spell *wind*; if he is unsure, allow him to look at the word.

Math: Work on your selected math curriculum for 15–20 minutes.

Science: In your SCM science course, complete the second assignment for Week 21.

Lesson 106

Materials Needed
- *A Child's Copybook Reader, Volume 2* (Track A)
- *More New Friends* (Track B)
- Math course of choice
- *Journaling a Year in Nature* notebooks (optional)

Track A: Have your student carefully copy the rest of the sentence in *A Child's Copybook Reader, Volume 2,* beginning on page 46: "but it did not fall, because it had been founded on the rock." When he has finished the copywork, invite him to spell any word he remembers. Ask him to spell *been*; if he is unsure, allow him to look at the word. See if he can also spell *rock*.

Track B: Have your student read aloud *More New Friends*, pages 88–95, "Two Thankful Girls."

Math: Work on your selected math curriculum for 15–20 minutes.

Notes

Nature Study: Take the whole family outside for nature study.

Lesson 107

Materials Needed
- Math course of choice
- *A Child's Copybook Reader, Volume 2* (Track A)
- *More Busy Times* (Track A)
- *Print to Cursive Proverbs* (Track B)

Math: Work on your selected math curriculum for 15–20 minutes.

Track A: Have your student read aloud *A Child's Copybook Reader, Volume 2,* page 48.

Help your student read aloud *More Busy Times,* pages 27–38, "A Special Day."

Tip: Do the math lesson between the two Track A assignments to break up the back-to-back readings. (See tip on lesson 3.)

Track B: Have your student read aloud the proverb at the top of *Print to Cursive Proverbs,* page 80, then copy the first phrase: "Do not rejoice when your enemy falls,". When he has finished the copywork, invite him to spell any word he remembers. Ask him to spell *when;* if he is unsure, allow him to look at the word.

Lesson 108

Materials Needed
- *A Child's Copybook Reader, Volume 2* (Track A)
- *Print to Cursive Proverbs* (Track B)
- Math course of choice
- SCM science course of choice

Track A: Have your student carefully copy the first part of the next sentence in the Scripture passage in *A Child's Copybook Reader, Volume 2,* beginning on page 49: "And everyone who hears these words of mine and does not do them." When he has finished the copywork, invite him to spell any word he remembers. Ask him to spell *words;* if he is unsure, allow him to look at the word.

Track B: Have your student read aloud the proverb at the top of *Print to Cursive Proverbs,* page 80, then copy the rest of the proverb on pages 81 and the top of 82.

Math: Work on your selected math curriculum for 15–20 minutes.

Science: In your SCM science course, complete the first assignment for Week 22.

Lesson 109

Materials Needed
- *A Child's Copybook Reader, Volume 2* (Track A)
- *More New Friends* (Track B)
- Math course of choice

Track A: Have your student carefully copy the rest of the sentence in *A Child's Copybook Reader, Volume 2,* beginning on page 50: "will be like a foolish man who built his house on the sand." When he has finished the copywork, invite him to spell any word he remembers. Ask him to spell *will*; if he is unsure, allow him to look at the word.

Track B: Have your student read aloud *More New Friends,* pages 96–105, "Vacation for Mother."

Math: Work on your selected math curriculum for 15–20 minutes.

Lesson 110

Materials Needed
- *More Busy Times* (Track A)
- *Print to Cursive Proverbs* (Track B)
- Math course of choice
- SCM science course of choice

Track A: Help your student read aloud *More Busy Times*, pages 39–50, "Grandfather Plays Doctor."

Track B: Have your student complete the rest of *Print to Cursive Proverbs*, page 82. When he has finished the copywork, invite him to spell any word he remembers. Ask him to spell *farm*; if he is unsure, allow him to look at the word.

Math: Work on your selected math curriculum for 15–20 minutes.

Science: In your SCM science course, complete the second assignment for Week 22.

Lesson 111

Materials Needed
- *A Child's Copybook Reader, Volume 2* (Track A)
- *More New Friends* (Track B)
- Math course of choice
- *Journaling a Year in Nature* notebooks (optional)

Track A: Have your student carefully copy the first part of the next sentence of the Scripture passage in *A Child's Copybook Reader, Volume 2*, beginning on page 51: "And the rain fell, and the floods came, and the winds blew and beat against that house." When he has finished the copywork, invite him to spell any word he remembers. Ask him to spell *came*; if he is unsure, allow him to look at the word.

Track B: Have your student read aloud *More New Friends,* pages 105–116, "A Happy, Busy Day."

Math: Work on your selected math curriculum for 15–20 minutes.

Nature Study: Take the whole family outside for nature study.

Reminder: Get A Child's Copybook Reader, Volume 3, *for Track A for lesson 121.*

Lesson 112

Materials Needed
- Math course of choice
- *A Child's Copybook Reader, Volume 2* (Track A)
- *More Busy Times*, if needed (Track A)
- *Print to Cursive Proverbs* (Track B)

Math: Work on your selected math curriculum for 15–20 minutes.

Track A: Have your student carefully copy the rest of the sentence in *A Child's Copybook Reader, Volume 2*, beginning on page 52: "and it fell, and great was the fall of it." When he has finished the copywork, invite him to spell any word he remembers. Ask him to spell *fall*; if he is unsure, allow him to look at the word. See if he can also spell *fell*.

Use today to catch up on any assigned reading in *More Busy Times*, as needed.

Track B: Have your student read aloud the proverb at the top of *Print to Cursive Proverbs*, page 83, then copy the first part: "The reward for humility and fear of the Lord."

Lesson 113

Materials Needed
- *A Child's Copybook Reader, Volume 2* (Track A)
- *Print to Cursive Proverbs* (Track B)
- Math course of choice
- SCM science course of choice

Track A: Have your student read aloud the Scripture passage in *A Child's Copybook Reader, Volume 2*, page 54, then carefully copy the first phrase of the passage on page 55: "And when Jesus finished these sayings,". When he has finished the copywork, invite him to spell any word he remembers. Ask him to spell *Jesus*; if he is unsure, allow him to look at the word.

Track B: Have your student read aloud the proverb at the top of *Print to Cursive Proverbs*, page 83, then copy the rest of the proverb on pages 84 and the top of 85. When he has finished the copywork, invite him to spell any word he remembers. Ask him to spell *riches*; if he is unsure, allow him to look at the word.

Math: Work on your selected math curriculum for 15–20 minutes.

Science: In your SCM science course, complete the first assignment for Week 23.

Lesson 114

Materials Needed
- *A Child's Copybook Reader, Volume 2* (Track A)
- *More New Friends*, if needed (Track B)
- Math course of choice

Track A: Have your student carefully copy the next phrase of the passage in *A Child's Copybook Reader, Volume 2*, beginning on page 55: "the crowds were astonished at his teaching,". When he has finished the copywork, invite him to spell any word he remembers. Ask him to spell *were*; if he is unsure, allow him to look at the word. See if he can also spell *when*.

Track B: Use today and lessons 116 and 119 to catch up on any assigned reading in *More New Friends*, as needed.

Math: Work on your selected math curriculum for 15–20 minutes.

Lesson 115

Materials Needed
- *More Busy Times* (Track A)
- *Print to Cursive Proverbs* (Track B)
- Math course of choice
- SCM science course of choice

Track A: Help your student read aloud *More Busy Times*, pages 51–64, "Another Special Day."

Track B: Have your student complete the rest of *Print to Cursive Proverbs*, page 85. When he has finished the copywork, invite him to spell any word he remembers. Ask him to spell *why*; if he is unsure, allow him to look at the word.

Math: Work on your selected math curriculum for 15–20 minutes.

Science: In your SCM science course, complete the second assignment for Week 23.

Lesson 116

Materials Needed
- *A Child's Copybook Reader, Volume 2* (Track A)
- *More New Friends*, if needed (Track B)
- Math course of choice
- *Journaling a Year in Nature* notebooks (optional)

Track A: Have your student carefully copy the rest of the Scripture passage in *A Child's Copybook Reader, Volume 2*, beginning on page 56. When he has finished the copywork, invite him to spell any word he remembers. Ask him to spell *for*; if he is unsure, allow him to look at the word.

Track B: Use today and lesson 119 to catch up on any assigned reading in *More New Friends*, as needed.

Math: Work on your selected math curriculum for 15–20 minutes.

Nature Study: Take the whole family outside for nature study.

Lesson 117

Materials Needed
- Math course of choice
- *A Child's Copybook Reader, Volume 2* (Track A)
- *Print to Cursive Proverbs* (Track B)

Math: Work on your selected math curriculum for 15–20 minutes.

Track A: Have your student read aloud the Scripture passage in *A Child's Copybook Reader, Volume 2*, on page 58. If desired, review 6–10 of these words and his selected words from previous copywork lessons: *then, who, rain, been, rock, words, will, came, fell, fall, Jesus, were, when, for.* If your student is unsure about a particular word's spelling, allow him to look at the word.

Track B: Have your student read aloud the proverb at the top of *Print to Cursive Proverbs*, page 86, then copy the first part: "Whoever is slow to anger has great understanding,".

Lesson 118

Materials Needed
- *A Child's Copybook Reader, Volume 2*, if needed (Track A)

- *More Busy Times* (Track A)
- *Print to Cursive Proverbs* (Track B)
- Math course of choice
- SCM science course of choice

Track A: Use today and tomorrow to catch up on any assigned reading and writing in *A Child's Copybook Reader, Volume 2*, as needed. If desired, review 6–10 of these words and his selected words from copywork lessons in Term 1: *and, all, things, them, each, that, made, their, in, at, God, the, running, sunset, up, winter, summer, garden, one, trees, we, water, day, see, tell, is, has, had, two, but, look, get, by, down, this, like.* If your student is unsure about a particular word's spelling, allow him to look at the word.

Help your student read aloud *More Busy Times*, pages 66–75, "The Wolf Story."

Track B: Have your student read aloud the proverb at the top of *Print to Cursive Proverbs*, page 86, then copy the rest of pages 87 and 88. When he has finished the copywork, invite him to spell any word he remembers. Ask him to spell *who*; if he is unsure, allow him to look at the word.

Math: Work on your selected math curriculum for 15–20 minutes.

Science: In your SCM science course, complete the first assignment for Week 24.

Lesson 119

Materials Needed
- *A Child's Copybook Reader, Volume 2,* if needed (Track A)
- *More New Friends*, if needed (Track B)
- Math course of choice

Track A: Use today to catch up on any assigned reading and writing in *A Child's Copybook Reader, Volume 2*, as needed. If desired, review 6–10 of these words and his selected words from copywork lessons in Term 2: *other, my, out, think, its, go, was, play, so, about, her, said, love, did, you, with, on, his, boys, they, are, cart, he, to, digs, pigs, last, do, much.* If your student is unsure about a particular word's spelling, allow him to look at the word.

Track B: Use today to catch up on any assigned reading in *More New Friends*, as needed.

Math: Work on your selected math curriculum for 15–20 minutes.

Lesson 120

Materials Needed
- *More Busy Times* (Track A)
- *Print to Cursive Proverbs*, if needed (Track B)

- Math course of choice
- SCM science course of choice

Track A: Help your student read aloud *More Busy Times*, pages 76–86, "The Doll Story."

Track B: Use today to catch up on any assigned pages in *Print to Cursive Proverbs*, as needed. If desired, review these words and your student's selected words from previous copywork lessons: *water, quick, wind, when, farm, riches, why, who*. If your student is unsure about a particular word's spelling, allow him to look at the word.

Math: Work on your selected math curriculum for 15–20 minutes.

Science: In your SCM science course, complete the second assignment for Week 24.

Term 3

(12 weeks; 5 lessons/week)

Term 3 Resources List

- Math course of choice
- Simply Charlotte Mason (SCM) science course of choice
- *Journaling a Year in Nature* notebooks (optional)

Track A

- *A Child's Copybook Reader, Volume 3*
- *More Busy Times*

Track B

- *Print to Cursive Proverbs*
- *More New Friends*

Weekly Schedule

	Day One	Day Two	Day Three	Day Four	Day Five
	Math (15–20 min.)	Math (15–20 min.)	Math (15–20 min.)	Math (15–20 min.)	Math (15–20 min.)
		Science (15–20 min.)		(Nature Study)	Science (15–20 min.)
Track A	Copybook Reader (5 min.)	More Busy Times (10–15 min.)	Copybook Reader (5 min.)	More Busy Times (10–15 min.)	Copybook Reader (5 min.)
Track B	More New Friends (10–15 min.)	Print to Cursive Proverbs (5–10 min.)	More New Friends (10–15 min.)		Print to Cursive Proverbs (5–10 min.)

Lesson 121

Materials Needed
- Math course of choice
- *A Child's Copybook Reader, Volume 3* (Track A)
- *More New Friends* (Track B)

Math: Work on your selected math curriculum for 15–20 minutes.

Track A: Have your student read aloud the stanza in *A Child's Copybook Reader, Volume 3*, page 4, then carefully copy the first two lines of that stanza on pages 5 and top of 6: "The wise may bring their learning, the rich may bring their wealth,". When he has finished the copywork, invite him to spell any word he remembers. Ask him to spell *bring*; if he is unsure, allow him to look at the word.

Track B: Have your student read aloud *More New Friends*, pages 118–127, "Slow Feet."

Lesson 122

Materials Needed
- SCM science course of choice
- Math course of choice
- *More Busy Times* (Track A)
- *Print to Cursive Proverbs* (Track B)

Science: In your SCM science course, complete the first assignment for Week 25.

Math: Work on your selected math curriculum for 15–20 minutes.

Track A: Help your student read aloud *More Busy Times*, pages 87–99, "The Doll Story (part 2)."

Track B: Have your student read aloud the proverb at the top of *Print to Cursive Proverbs*, page 89, then copy the first part: "A tranquil heart gives life to the flesh,".

Lesson 123

Materials Needed
- Math course of choice
- *A Child's Copybook Reader, Volume 3* (Track A)
- *More New Friends* (Track B)

Math: Work on your selected math curriculum for 15–20 minutes.

Track A: Have your student carefully copy the rest of the stanza in *A Child's*

Copybook Reader, Volume 3, pages 6 and 7. When he has finished the copywork, invite him to spell any word he remembers. Ask him to spell *some*; if he is unsure, allow him to look at the word. See if he can also spell *come*.

Track B: Have your student read aloud *More New Friends*, pages 127–142, "Singing Wheels."

Lesson 124

Materials Needed
- Math course of choice
- *More Busy Times*, if needed (Track A)
- *Journaling a Year in Nature* notebooks (optional)

Math: Work on your selected math curriculum for 15–20 minutes.

Track A: Use today to catch up on any assigned reading in *More Busy Times*, as needed.

Nature Study: Take the whole family outside for nature study.

Lesson 125

Materials Needed
- SCM science course of choice
- Math course of choice
- *A Child's Copybook Reader, Volume 3* (Track A)
- *Print to Cursive Proverbs* (Track B)

Science: In your SCM science course, complete the second assignment for Week 25.

Math: Work on your selected math curriculum for 15–20 minutes.

Track A: Have your student read aloud the stanza in *A Child's Copybook Reader, Volume 3*, page 8, then carefully copy page 9. When he has finished the copywork, invite him to spell any word he remembers. Ask him to spell *would*; if he is unsure, allow him to look at the word. See if he can also spell *could*.

Track B: Have your student read aloud the proverb at the top of *Print to Cursive Proverbs*, page 89, then copy the rest of page 90. When he has finished the copywork, invite him to spell any word he remembers. Ask him to spell *bones*; if he is unsure, allow him to look at the word.

Lesson 126

Materials Needed
- Math course of choice

- *A Child's Copybook Reader, Volume 3* (Track A)
- *More New Friends* (Track B)

Math: Work on your selected math curriculum for 15–20 minutes.

Track A: Have your student carefully copy the rest of the stanza in *A Child's Copybook Reader, Volume 3*, pages 10 and 11. When he has finished the copywork, invite him to spell any word he remembers. Ask him to spell *or*; if he is unsure, allow him to look at the word. See if he can also spell *no*.

Track B: Have your student read aloud *More New Friends*, pages 142–151, "The Lost Billfold."

Lesson 127

Materials Needed
- SCM science course of choice
- Math course of choice
- *More Busy Times* (Track A)
- *Print to Cursive Proverbs* (Track B)

Science: In your SCM science course, complete the first assignment for Week 26.

Math: Work on your selected math curriculum for 15–20 minutes.

Track A: Help your student read aloud *More Busy Times*, pages 100–113, "The Grandmother Story."

Track B: Have your student complete *Print to Cursive Proverbs*, page 91. When he has finished the copywork, invite him to spell any word he remembers. Ask him to spell *love*; if he is unsure, allow him to look at the word.

Lesson 128

Materials Needed
- Math course of choice
- *A Child's Copybook Reader, Volume 3* (Track A)
- *More New Friends* (Track B)

Math: Work on your selected math curriculum for 15–20 minutes.

Track A: Have your student read aloud the stanza in *A Child's Copybook Reader, Volume 3*, page 12, then carefully copy the first two lines of that stanza on pages 13 and top of 14: "We'll bring Him hearts that love Him; we'll bring Him thankful praise,". Point out the word *we'll* and its apostrophe. Explain that it stands for *we will*. When he has finished the copywork, invite him to spell any word he remembers. Ask him to spell *we'll*; if he is unsure, allow him to look at the word.

Track B: Have your student read aloud *More New Friends*, pages 152–164, "The Wrong Reward."

Lesson 129

Materials Needed
- Math course of choice
- *More Busy Times* (Track A)
- *Journaling a Year in Nature* notebooks (optional)

Math: Work on your selected math curriculum for 15–20 minutes.

Track A: Help your student read aloud *More Busy Times*, pages 114–124, "The Finders-Keepers Story."

Nature Study: Take the whole family outside for nature study.

Lesson 130

Materials Needed
- SCM science course of choice
- Math course of choice
- *A Child's Copybook Reader, Volume 3* (Track A)
- *Print to Cursive Proverbs* (Track B)

Science: In your SCM science course, complete the second assignment for Week 26.

Math: Work on your selected math curriculum for 15–20 minutes.

Track A: Have your student carefully copy the rest of the stanza in *A Child's Copybook Reader, Volume 3,* pages 14 and 15. When he has finished the copywork, invite him to spell any word he remembers. Ask him to spell *ways*; if he is unsure, allow him to look at the word.

Track B: Have your student read aloud the proverb at the top of *Print to Cursive Proverbs*, page 92, then copy the first part: "Like the glaze covering an earthen vessel".

Lesson 131

Materials Needed
- Math course of choice
- *A Child's Copybook Reader, Volume 3* (Track A)
- *More New Friends*, if needed (Track B)

Math: Work on your selected math curriculum for 15–20 minutes.

Track A: Have your student read aloud the stanza in *A Child's Copybook Reader, Volume 3*, page 16, then carefully copy page 17. When he has finished the copywork, invite him to spell any word he remembers. Ask him to spell *be*; if he is unsure, allow him to look at the word.

Track B: Use today to catch up on any assigned reading in *More New Friends*, as needed.

Lesson 132

Materials Needed
- SCM science course of choice
- Math course of choice
- *More Busy Times* (Track A)
- *Print to Cursive Proverbs* (Track B)

Science: In your SCM science course, complete the first assignment for Week 27.

Math: Work on your selected math curriculum for 15–20 minutes.

Track A: Help your student read aloud *More Busy Times*, pages 126–136, "The Smallest Girl."

Track B: Have your student read aloud the proverb at the top of *Print to Cursive Proverbs*, page 92, then copy the rest of page 93. When he has finished the copywork, invite him to spell any word he remembers. Ask him to spell *evil*; if he is unsure, allow him to look at the word.

Lesson 133

Materials Needed
- Math course of choice
- *A Child's Copybook Reader, Volume 3* (Track A)
- *More New Friends* (Track B)

Math: Work on your selected math curriculum for 15–20 minutes.

Track A: Have your student carefully copy *A Child's Copybook Reader, Volume 3*, page 18. When he has finished the copywork, invite him to spell any word he remembers. Ask him to spell *may*; if he is unsure, allow him to look at the word.

Track B: Have your student read aloud *More New Friends*, pages 166–175, "Funny Face."

Lesson 134

Materials Needed
- Math course of choice
- *More Busy Times* (Track A)
- *Journaling a Year in Nature* notebooks (optional)

Math: Work on your selected math curriculum for 15–20 minutes.

Track A: Help your student read aloud *More Busy Times*, pages 137–148, "A Hard Day for Nancy."

Nature Study: Take the whole family outside for nature study.

Lesson 135

Materials Needed
- SCM science course of choice
- Math course of choice
- *A Child's Copybook Reader, Volume 3* (Track A)
- *Print to Cursive Proverbs* (Track B)

Science: In your SCM science course, complete the second assignment for Week 27.

Math: Work on your selected math curriculum for 15–20 minutes.

Track A: Have your student read aloud the stanza in *A Child's Copybook Reader, Volume 3,* page 19, then carefully copy page 20. When he has finished the copywork, invite him to spell any word he remembers. Ask him to spell *have*; if he is unsure, allow him to look at the word.

Track B: Have your student complete *Print to Cursive Proverbs*, page 94. When he has finished the copywork, invite him to spell any word he remembers. Ask him to spell *size*; if he is unsure, allow him to look at the word.

Lesson 136

Materials Needed
- Math course of choice
- *A Child's Copybook Reader, Volume 3* (Track A)
- *More New Friends* (Track B)

Math: Work on your selected math curriculum for 15–20 minutes.

Track A: Have your student carefully copy *A Child's Copybook Reader, Volume 3*, page 21. When he has finished the copywork, invite him to spell any word he remembers. Ask him to spell *him*; if he is unsure, allow him to look at the word.

Track B: Have your student read aloud *More New Friends*, pages 175–183, "A Trip to Town."

Lesson 137

Materials Needed
- SCM science course of choice
- Math course of choice
- *More Busy Times*, if needed (Track A)
- *Print to Cursive Proverbs*, if needed (Track B)

Science: In your SCM science course, complete the first assignment for Week 28.

Math: Work on your selected math curriculum for 15–20 minutes.

Track A: Use today to catch up on any assigned reading in *More Busy Times*, as needed.

Track B: Use today to catch up on any assigned pages in *Print to Cursive Proverbs*, as needed. If desired, review these words and your student's selected words from previous copywork lessons: *bones, love, evil, size.* If your student is unsure about a particular word's spelling, allow him to look at the word.

Lesson 138

Materials Needed
- Math course of choice
- *A Child's Copybook Reader, Volume 3* (Track A)
- *More New Friends* (Track B)

Math: Work on your selected math curriculum for 15–20 minutes.

Track A: Have your student read aloud the stanza in *A Child's Copybook Reader, Volume 3*, page 22, then carefully copy page 23. When he has finished the copywork, invite him to spell any word he remembers. Ask him to spell *these*; if he is unsure, allow him to look at the word.

Track B: Have your student read aloud *More New Friends*, pages 184–191, "Spoiled Plans."

Lesson 139

Materials Needed
- Math course of choice
- *More Busy Times* (Track A)
- *Journaling a Year in Nature* notebooks (optional)

Math: Work on your selected math curriculum for 15–20 minutes.

Track A: Help your student read aloud *More Busy Times*, pages 149–156, "Nelson's Problem."

Nature Study: Take the whole family outside for nature study.

Lesson 140

Materials Needed
- SCM science course of choice
- Math course of choice
- *A Child's Copybook Reader, Volume 3* (Track A)
- *Print to Cursive Proverbs* (Track B)

Science: In your SCM science course, complete the second assignment for Week 28.

Math: Work on your selected math curriculum for 15–20 minutes.

Track A: Have your student carefully copy *A Child's Copybook Reader, Volume 3*, page 24. When he has finished the copywork, invite him to spell any word he remembers. Ask him to spell *than*; if he is unsure, allow him to look at the word. Discuss how it is different from *then* in both spelling and meaning.

Track B: Have your student complete *Print to Cursive Proverbs*, page 95.

Lesson 141

Materials Needed
- Math course of choice
- *A Child's Copybook Reader, Volume 3* (Track A)
- *More New Friends* (Track B)

Math: Work on your selected math curriculum for 15–20 minutes.

Track A: Have your student read aloud the entire poem in *A Child's Copybook Reader, Volume 3*, page 25. If desired, review 6–10 of these words and his selected words from previous copywork lessons: *bring, some, come, would, could, or, no, we'll, ways, be, may, have, him, these, than*. If your student is unsure about a particular word's spelling, allow him to look at the word.

Track B: Have your student read aloud *More New Friends*, pages 191–199, "A New Game."

Lesson 142

Materials Needed
- SCM science course of choice
- Math course of choice
- *More Busy Times* (Track A)
- *Print to Cursive Proverbs* (Track B)

Science: In your SCM science course, complete the first assignment for Week 29.

Math: Work on your selected math curriculum for 15–20 minutes.

Track A: Help your student read aloud *More Busy Times*, pages 157–170, "Nelson and Dr. Wood."

Track B: Have your student complete *Print to Cursive Proverbs*, page 96. When he has finished the copywork, invite him to spell any word he remembers. Ask him to spell *even*; if he is unsure, allow him to look at the word.

Tip: It is up to your discretion whether you want to require/review how to form the uppercase letter at the beginning of the words that you will ask your student to spell from memory throughout the rest of the Print to Cursive *lessons. Of course, if you are checking the words' spellings orally, it won't matter.*

Lesson 143

Materials Needed
- Math course of choice
- *A Child's Copybook Reader, Volume 3* (Track A)
- *More New Friends*, if needed (Track B)

Math: Work on your selected math curriculum for 15–20 minutes.

Track A: Have your student read aloud the paragraph in *A Child's Copybook Reader, Volume 3*, page 27, then carefully copy its first sentence on pages 28 and 29. When he has finished the copywork, invite him to spell any word he remembers. Ask him to spell *if*; if he is unsure, allow him to look at the word. See if he can also spell *from*.

Tip: You may want to draw your student's attention to the period at the top of page 29 as the signal of the end of that sentence.

Track B: Use today to catch up on any assigned reading in *More New Friends*, as needed.

Lesson 144

Materials Needed
- Math course of choice
- *More Busy Times* (Track A)
- *Journaling a Year in Nature* notebooks (optional)

Math: Work on your selected math curriculum for 15–20 minutes.

Track A: Help your student read aloud *More Busy Times*, pages 172–182, "Peter's Bank."

Nature Study: Take the whole family outside for nature study.

Lesson 145

Materials Needed
- SCM science course of choice
- Math course of choice
- *A Child's Copybook Reader, Volume 3* (Track A)
- *Print to Cursive Proverbs* (Track B)

Science: In your SCM science course, complete the second assignment for Week 29.

Math: Work on your selected math curriculum for 15–20 minutes.

Track A: Have your student carefully copy the next sentence of the paragraph in *A Child's Copybook Reader, Volume 3,* pages 29 and 30: "The dog barks as a cart passes by, rumbling." When he has finished the copywork, invite him to spell any word he remembers. Ask him to spell *barks*; if he is unsure, allow him to look at the word.

Track B: Have your student complete *Print to Cursive Proverbs*, page 97. When he has finished the copywork, invite him to spell any word he remembers. Ask him to spell *father*; if he is unsure, allow him to look at the word.

Lesson 146

Materials Needed
- Math course of choice
- *A Child's Copybook Reader, Volume 3* (Track A)
- *More New Friends* (Track B)

Math: Work on your selected math curriculum for 15–20 minutes.

Track A: Have your student carefully copy the next sentence of the paragraph in *A Child's Copybook Reader, Volume 3,* page 30: "The carter whistles and cracks his whip." When he has finished the copywork, invite him to spell any word he remembers. Ask him to spell *whip*; if he is unsure, allow him to look at the word.

Track B: Have your student read aloud *More New Friends*, pages 201–209, "The Wooden Box."

Lesson 147

Materials Needed
- SCM science course of choice
- Math course of choice
- *More Busy Times* (Track A)
- *Print to Cursive Proverbs* (Track B)

Science: In your SCM science course, complete the first assignment for Week 30.

Math: Work on your selected math curriculum for 15–20 minutes.

Track A: Help your student read aloud *More Busy Times*, pages 183–191, "Peter Learns a Lesson."

Track B: Have your student complete *Print to Cursive Proverbs*, page 98. When he has finished the copywork, invite him to spell any word he remembers. Ask him to spell *hear*; if he is unsure, allow him to look at the word.

Lesson 148

Materials Needed
- Math course of choice
- *A Child's Copybook Reader, Volume 3* (Track A)
- *More New Friends* (Track B)

Math: Work on your selected math curriculum for 15–20 minutes.

Track A: Have your student carefully copy the last sentence of the paragraph in *A Child's Copybook Reader, Volume 3*, pages 30–32. When he has finished the copywork, invite him to spell any word he remembers. Ask him to spell *as*; if he is unsure, allow him to look at the word.

Track B: Have your student read aloud *More New Friends*, pages 209–218, "A Surprise for Toby."

Lesson 149

Materials Needed
- Math course of choice
- *More Busy Times*, if needed (Track A)

Notes

• *Journaling a Year in Nature* notebooks (optional)

Math: Work on your selected math curriculum for 15–20 minutes.

Track A: Use today to catch up on any assigned reading in *More Busy Times*, as needed.

Nature Study: Take the whole family outside for nature study.

Lesson 150

Materials Needed
• SCM science course of choice
• Math course of choice
• *A Child's Copybook Reader, Volume 3* (Track A)
• *Print to Cursive Proverbs* (Track B)

Science: In your SCM science course, complete the second assignment for Week 30.

Math: Work on your selected math curriculum for 15–20 minutes.

Track A: Have your student read aloud the paragraph in *A Child's Copybook Reader, Volume 3*, page 33, then carefully copy its first two clauses on pages 34 and 35: "The wind whispers in the fir branches; the birds sing in them;". When he has finished the copywork, invite him to spell any word he remembers. Ask him to spell *birds*; if he is unsure, allow him to look at the word.

Track B: Have your student complete *Print to Cursive Proverbs*, page 99. When he has finished the copywork, invite him to spell any word he remembers. Ask him to spell *keep*; if he is unsure, allow him to look at the word.

Lesson 151

Materials Needed
• Math course of choice
• *A Child's Copybook Reader, Volume 3* (Track A)
• *More New Friends* (Track B)

Math: Work on your selected math curriculum for 15–20 minutes.

Track A: Have your student carefully copy the rest of that sentence and the next in *A Child's Copybook Reader, Volume 3,* pages 35 and 36: "and the cat purrs, sitting under them. Dan chops up the logs." When he has finished the copywork, invite him to spell any word he remembers. Ask him to spell *under*; if he is unsure, allow him to look at the word.

Track B: Have your student read aloud *More New Friends*, pages 219–226, "Toby and the Teaser."

Lesson 152

Materials Needed
- SCM science course of choice
- Math course of choice
- *More Busy Times* (Track A)
- *Print to Cursive Proverbs* (Track B)

Science: In your SCM science course, complete the first assignment for Week 31.

Math: Work on your selected math curriculum for 15–20 minutes.

Track A: Help your student read aloud *More Busy Times*, pages 192–200, "Peter Finds a Way."

Track B: Have your student complete *Print to Cursive Proverbs*, page 100. When he has finished the copywork, invite him to spell any word he remembers. Ask him to spell *queen*; if he is unsure, allow him to look at the word.

Lesson 153

Materials Needed
- Math course of choice
- *A Child's Copybook Reader, Volume 3* (Track A)
- *More New Friends* (Track B)

Math: Work on your selected math curriculum for 15–20 minutes.

Track A: Have your student carefully copy the last sentence of the paragraph in *A Child's Copybook Reader, Volume 3*, pages 36 and 37. When he has finished the copywork, invite him to spell any word he remembers. Ask him to spell *number*; if he is unsure, allow him to look at the word. See if he can also spell *of*.

Track B: Have your student read aloud *More New Friends*, pages 226–233, "Billy Bouncer."

Lesson 154

Materials Needed
- Math course of choice
- *More Busy Times* (Track A)
- *Journaling a Year in Nature* notebooks (optional)

Math: Work on your selected math curriculum for 15–20 minutes.

Track A: Help your student read aloud *More Busy Times*, pages 201–211, "Trapping Mice."

Notes

Nature Study: Take the whole family outside for nature study.

Lesson 155

Materials Needed
- SCM science course of choice
- Math course of choice
- *A Child's Copybook Reader, Volume 3* (Track A)
- *Print to Cursive Proverbs* (Track B)

Science: In your SCM science course, complete the second assignment for Week 31.

Math: Work on your selected math curriculum for 15–20 minutes.

Track A: Have your student read aloud the paragraph in *A Child's Copybook Reader, Volume 3*, page 38, then carefully copy its first sentence on pages 39 and top of 40. When he has finished the copywork, invite him to spell any word he remembers. Ask him to spell *grass*; if he is unsure, allow him to look at the word.

Track B: Have your student complete *Print to Cursive Proverbs*, page 101. When he has finished the copywork, invite him to spell any word he remembers. Ask him to spell *Rachel*; if he is unsure, allow him to look at the word.

Lesson 156

Materials Needed
- Math course of choice
- *A Child's Copybook Reader, Volume 3* (Track A)
- *More New Friends* (Track B)

Math: Work on your selected math curriculum for 15–20 minutes.

Track A: Have your student carefully copy the next sentence in *A Child's Copybook Reader, Volume 3,* pages 40 and 41. When he has finished the copywork, invite him to spell any word he remembers. Ask him to spell *ducks*; if he is unsure, allow him to look at the word. See if he can also spell *fish*.

Track B: Have you student read aloud *More New Friends*, pages 233–240, "Toby Tries."

Lesson 157

Materials Needed
- SCM science course of choice
- Math course of choice
- *More Busy Times* (Track A)

- *Print to Cursive Proverbs* (Track B)

Science: In your SCM science course, complete the first assignment for Week 32.

Math: Work on your selected math curriculum for 15–20 minutes.

Track A: Help your student read aloud *More Busy Times,* pages 212–226, "A Trap for Peter."

Track B: Have your student complete *Print to Cursive Proverbs*, page 102. When he has finished the copywork, invite him to spell any word he remembers. Ask him to spell *better*; if he is unsure, allow him to look at the word.

Lesson 158

Materials Needed
- Math course of choice
- *A Child's Copybook Reader, Volume 3* (Track A)
- *More New Friends,* if needed (Track B)

Math: Work on your selected math curriculum for 15–20 minutes.

Track A: Have your student carefully copy the last sentence of the paragraph in *A Child's Copybook Reader, Volume 3,* pages 41 and 42. When he has finished the copywork, invite him to spell any word he remembers. Ask him to spell *little*; if he is unsure, allow him to look at the word.

Track B: Use today to catch up on any assigned reading in *More New Friends,* as needed.

Lesson 159

Materials Needed
- Math course of choice
- *More Busy Times,* if needed (Track A)
- *Journaling a Year in Nature* notebooks (optional)

Math: Work on your selected math curriculum for 15–20 minutes.

Track A: Use today to catch up on any assigned reading in *More Busy Times,* as needed.

Nature Study: Take the whole family outside for nature study.

Lesson 160

Materials Needed
- SCM science course of choice

Notes

- Math course of choice
- *A Child's Copybook Reader, Volume 3* (Track A)
- *Print to Cursive Proverbs* (Track B)

Science: In your SCM science course, complete the second assignment for Week 32.

Math: Work on your selected math curriculum for 15–20 minutes.

Track A: Have your student read aloud the sentence in *A Child's Copybook Reader, Volume 3,* page 43, then carefully copy it on pages 44 and 45. When he has finished the copywork, invite him to spell any word he remembers. Ask him to spell *into*; if he is unsure, allow him to look at the word.

Track B: Have your student complete *Print to Cursive Proverbs,* page 103. When he has finished the copywork, invite him to spell any word he remembers. Ask him to spell *Joshua*; if he is unsure, allow him to look at the word.

Lesson 161

Materials Needed
- Math course of choice
- *A Child's Copybook Reader, Volume 3* (Track A)
- *More New Friends* (Track B)

Math: Work on your selected math curriculum for 15–20 minutes.

Track A: Have your student read aloud the entire story in *A Child's Copybook Reader, Volume 3,* page 46. If desired, review 6–10 of these words and his selected words from previous copywork lessons: *if, from, barks, birds, whip, as, under, number, of, grass, ducks, fish, little, into.* If your student is unsure about a particular word's spelling, allow him to look at the word.

Track B: Have your student read aloud *More New Friends,* pages 242–253, "A Friend or an Enemy?"

Lesson 162

Materials Needed
- SCM science course of choice
- Math course of choice
- *More Busy Times* (Track A)
- *Print to Cursive Proverbs* (Track B)

Science: In your SCM science course, complete the first assignment for Week 33.

Math: Work on your selected math curriculum for 15–20 minutes.

Track A: Help your student read aloud *More Busy Times,* pages 228–238, "Susan and her Friends."

Track B: Have your student complete *Print to Cursive Proverbs,* page 104. When he has finished the copywork, invite him to spell any word he remembers. Ask him to spell *if;* if he is unsure, allow him to look at the word.

Lesson 163

Materials Needed
- Math course of choice
- *A Child's Copybook Reader, Volume 3* (Track A)
- *More New Friends* (Track B)

Math: Work on your selected math curriculum for 15–20 minutes.

Track A: Have your student read aloud the Scripture passage in *A Child's Copybook Reader, Volume 3,* page 48, then carefully copy the first part of it on pages 49 and 50: "Consider the lilies, how they grow: they neither toil nor spin,". When he has finished the copywork, invite him to spell any word he remembers. Ask him to spell *how;* if he is unsure, allow him to look at the word. See if he can also spell *now.*

Track B: Have your student read aloud *More New Friends,* pages 254–260, "Two Kinds of Fun."

Lesson 164

Materials Needed
- Math course of choice
- *More Busy Times* (Track A)
- *Journaling a Year in Nature* notebooks (optional)

Math: Work on your selected math curriculum for 15–20 minutes.

Track A: Help your student read aloud *More Busy Times,* pages 239–248, "A Friend for Susan."

Nature Study: Take the whole family outside for nature study.

Lesson 165

Materials Needed
- SCM science course of choice
- Math course of choice
- *A Child's Copybook Reader, Volume 3* (Track A)
- *Print to Cursive Proverbs* (Track B)

Science: In your SCM science course, complete the second assignment for Week 33.

Math: Work on your selected math curriculum for 15–20 minutes.

Track A: Have your student carefully copy the rest of the sentence in *A Child's Copybook Reader, Volume 3*, pages 50 and 51. When he has finished the copywork, invite him to spell any word he remembers. Ask him to spell *not*; if he is unsure, allow him to look at the word.

Track B: Have your student complete *Print to Cursive Proverbs*, page 105. When he has finished the copywork, invite him to spell any word he remembers. Ask him to spell *Samuel*; if he is unsure, allow him to look at the word.

Lesson 166

Materials Needed
- Math course of choice
- *A Child's Copybook Reader, Volume 3* (Track A)
- *More New Friends* (Track B)

Math: Work on your selected math curriculum for 15–20 minutes.

Track A: Have your student carefully copy more of the Scripture passage in *A Child's Copybook Reader, Volume 3,* beginning on page 51: "But if God so clothes the grass, which is alive in the field today, and tomorrow is thrown into the oven,". When he has finished the copywork, invite him to spell any word he remembers. Ask him to spell *which*; if he is unsure, allow him to look at the word.

Track B: Have your student read aloud *More New Friends,* pages 261–271, "Some Coals That Burn."

Lesson 167

Materials Needed
- SCM science course of choice
- Math course of choice
- *More Busy Times* (Track A)
- *Print to Cursive Proverbs* (Track B)

Science: In your SCM science course, complete the first assignment for Week 34.

Math: Work on your selected math curriculum for 15–20 minutes.

Track A: Help your student read aloud *More Busy Times,* pages 249–261, "Susan Tries."

Notes

Track B: Have your student complete *Print to Cursive Proverbs,* page 106. When he has finished the copywork, invite him to spell any word he remembers. Ask him to spell *Lord God*; if he is unsure, allow him to look at the word.

Lesson 168

Materials Needed
- Math course of choice
- *A Child's Copybook Reader, Volume 3* (Track A)
- *More New Friends* (Track B)

Math: Work on your selected math curriculum for 15–20 minutes.

Track A: Have your student carefully copy the rest of the Scripture passage in *A Child's Copybook Reader, Volume 3*, page 53. When he has finished the copywork, invite him to spell any word he remembers. Ask him to spell *more*; if he is unsure, allow him to look at the word.

Track B: Have your student read aloud *More New Friends,* pages 271–280, "A Narrow Escape."

Lesson 169

Materials Needed
- Math course of choice
- *More Busy Times* (Track A)
- *Journaling a Year in Nature* notebooks (optional)

Math: Work on your selected math curriculum for 15–20 minutes.

Track A: Help your student read aloud *More Busy Times*, pages 262–272, "Levi's Extra Fun."

Nature Study: Take the whole family outside for nature study.

Lesson 170

Materials Needed
- SCM science course of choice
- Math course of choice
- *A Child's Copybook Reader, Volume 3* (Track A)
- *Print to Cursive Proverbs* (Track B)

Science: In your SCM science course, complete the second assignment for Week 34.

Math: Work on your selected math curriculum for 15–20 minutes.

Track A: Have your student read aloud the Scripture passage in *A Child's Copybook Reader, Volume 3,* page 54.

Track B: Make 3–5 extra copies of page 107 before your student writes on it. (You will use the copies for some final lessons later.) Then have your student complete *Print to Cursive Proverbs*, page 107, by signing his name.

Lesson 171

Materials Needed
- Math course of choice
- *A Child's Copybook Reader, Volume 3* (Track A)
- *More New Friends* (Track B)

Math: Work on your selected math curriculum for 15–20 minutes.

Track A: Have your student carefully copy the first sentence of the Scripture passage in *A Child's Copybook Reader, Volume 3,* pages 55 and top of 56. When he has finished the copywork, invite him to spell any word he remembers. Ask him to spell *what*; if he is unsure, allow him to look at the word.

Track B: Have your student read aloud *More New Friends*, pages 280–285, "The Golden Windows."

Lesson 172

Materials Needed
- SCM science course of choice
- Math course of choice
- *More Busy Times* (Track A)
- *Print to Cursive Proverbs,* if needed (Track B)

Science: In your SCM science course, complete the first assignment for Week 35.

Math: Work on your selected math curriculum for 15–20 minutes.

Track A: Help your student read aloud *More Busy Times*, pages 273–285, "The Bobsled Bus."

Track B: Use today to catch up on any pages of *Print to Cursive Proverbs,* as needed.

Lesson 173

Materials Needed
- Math course of choice
- *A Child's Copybook Reader, Volume 3 (Track A)*

- *More New Friends,* if needed (Track B)

Math: Work on your selected math curriculum for 15–20 minutes.

Track A: Have your student carefully copy the next phrase of the Scripture passage in *A Child's Copybook Reader, Volume 3,* pages 56 and 57: "For all the nations of the world seek after these things,". When he has finished the copywork, invite him to spell any word he remembers. Ask him to spell *after*; if he is unsure, allow him to look at the word.

Track B: Use the rest of this week and next week to catch up on any assigned reading in *More New Friends,* as needed.

Lesson 174

Materials Needed
- Math course of choice
- *More Busy Times,* if needed (Track A)
- *Journaling a Year in Nature* notebooks (optional)

Math: Work on your selected math curriculum for 15–20 minutes.

Track A: Use today and next week to catch up on any assigned reading in *More Busy Times,* as needed.

Nature Study: Take the whole family outside for nature study.

Lesson 175

Materials Needed
- SCM science course of choice
- Math course of choice
- *A Child's Copybook Reader, Volume 3* (Track A)
- *Print to Cursive Proverbs* and copy of page 107 (Track B)

Science: In your SCM science course, complete the second assignment for Week 35.

Math: Work on your selected math curriculum for 15–20 minutes.

Track A: Have your student carefully copy *A Child's Copybook Reader, Volume 3,* the rest of page 57. When he has finished the copywork, invite him to spell any word he remembers. Ask him to spell *your*; if he is unsure, allow him to look at the word.

Track B: Have your student select any proverb from *Print to Cursive Proverbs* and write it in cursive. Use a copy of page 107 for your student to write on.

Lesson 176

Materials Needed
- Math course of choice
- *A Child's Copybook Reader, Volume 3* (Track A)
- *More New Friends,* if needed (Track B)

Math: Work on your selected math curriculum for 15–20 minutes.

Track A: Have your student carefully copy *A Child's Copybook Reader, Volume 3,* page 58. When he has finished the copywork, invite him to spell any word he remembers. Ask him to spell *seek*; if he is unsure, allow him to look at the word.

Track B: Use this week to catch up on any assigned reading in *More New Friends*, as needed.

Lesson 177

Materials Needed
- SCM science course of choice
- Math course of choice
- *More Busy Times,* if needed (Track A)
- *Print to Cursive Proverbs* and copy of page 107 (Track B)

Science: In your SCM science course, complete the first assignment for Week 36.

Math: Work on your selected math curriculum for 15–20 minutes.

Track A: Use this week to catch up on any assigned reading in *More Busy Times,* as needed.

Track B: Have your student select any proverb from *Print to Cursive Proverbs* and write it in cursive. Use a copy of page 107 for your student to write on.

Lesson 178

Materials Needed
- Math course of choice
- *A Child's Copybook Reader, Volume 3* (Track A)
- *More New Friends,* if needed (Track B)

Math: Work on your selected math curriculum for 15–20 minutes.

Track A: Have your student read aloud the Scripture passage in *A Child's Copybook Reader, Volume 3,* on page 59. If desired, review 6–10 of these words and his selected words from previous copywork lessons: *how, now, not, which, more, what, after, your, seek.* If your student is unsure about a particular word's spelling, allow him to look at the word.

Track B: Use today to catch up on any assigned reading in *More New Friends,* as needed.

Lesson 179

Materials Needed
- Math course of choice
- *More Busy Times,* if needed (Track A)
- *Journaling a Year in Nature* notebooks (optional)

Math: Work on your selected math curriculum for 15–20 minutes.

Track A: Use today to catch up on any assigned reading in *More Busy Times,* as needed.

Nature Study: Take the whole family outside for nature study.

Lesson 180

Materials Needed
- SCM science course of choice
- Math course of choice
- *A Child's Copybook Reader, Volume 3,* if needed (Track A)
- *Print to Cursive Proverbs* and copy of page 107 (Track B)

Science: In your SCM science course, complete the second assignment for Week 36.

Math: Work on your selected math curriculum for 15–20 minutes.

Track A: Use today to catch up on any assigned reading and writing in *A Child's Copybook Reader, Volume 3,* as needed. If desired, review 6–10 of these words and his selected words from copywork lessons in Term 3: *bring, some, come, would, could, or, no, we'll, ways, be, may, have, him, these, than, if, from, barks, whip, as, birds, under, number, of, grass, ducks, fish, little, into.* If your student is unsure about a particular word's spelling, allow him to look at the word.

Track B: Have your student select any proverb from *Print to Cursive Proverbs* and write it in cursive. Use a copy of page 107 for your student to write on.